# Urodynamics made easy

# Urodynamics made easy

**Christopher R. Chapple** BSc, FRCS
Senior Registrar in Urology, The Middlesex Hospital, London, UK

**Timothy J. Christmas** FRCS
Senior Registrar in Urology, St Bartholomews Hospital, London, UK

Foreword by

**Richard Trevor Turner-Warwick**
DSc, DM(Oxon), MCh, FRCP, FRCS, FRCOG, FACS, FRACS(Hon)
Senior Consultant Urological Surgeon, The Institute of Urology
and The Middlesex Hospital, London, UK

*Illustrations by* **Jane Fallows**

CHURCHILL LIVINGSTONE
EDINBURGH LONDON MELBOURNE AND NEW YORK 1990

CHURCHILL LIVINGSTONE
Medical Division of Longman Group UK Limited

Distributed in the United States of America by
Churchill Livingstone Inc., 1560 Broadway, New York,
NY 10036, and by associated companies, branches
and representatives throughout the world.

First published 1990

# ISBN 0-443-04503-8

**British Library Cataloguing in Publication Data**
  Urodynamics made easy.
  1. Urodynamics
  I. Chapple, Christopher R.    II. Christmas, Timothy J.
  616′2—dc20    RC901.9.U76

**Library of Congress Cataloging in Publication Data**
Urodynamics made easy
  Includes bibliographical references.    Includes index
  1. Urology    I. Chapple, Christopher R.    II. Christmas, Timothy J.
[DNLM: 1. Urinary Tract—physiology.
    2. Urinary tract—physiopathology.
    3. Urodynamics.    WJ 102 U779]
    RC901.9.U76    1990    616.6′2dc20    90-1984

Produced by Longman Singapore Publishers (Pte) Ltd.
Printed in Singapore

# Foreword

'When I use a word' said Humpty-Dumpty 'it means just what I choose it to mean—neither more nor less'—adding—'when I make a word do a lot of work I always pay it extra' (Lewis Carroll—*Alice Through The Looking Glass*).

To some extent most of us emulate Humpty-Dumpty in our use of words but many of us forget that others use them differently. Thus the North American concept of 'urodynamics' tends to be an electronic investigation that is conducted in a laboratory—usually without radiology and often by personnel who are not medically qualified. In Britain 'urodynamics' means the study or urinary tract function and dysfunction by any methods that are appropriate to the problem—whether clinical or academic. Thus the procedures required for the evaluation of a clinical problem may range from the simplest voided-volume chart (VVC)—a natural cystometrographic record of the individual volumes of urine voided over the period of 48 hours—to the synchronous video-pressure-flow-cystourethrogram (VPFCUG)—a sophisticated augmentation of the simple (and invaluable) voiding cystourethrogram (VCUG) that we developed in 1968 as a routine clinical procedure for the investigation of patients with complicated lower urinary tract dysfunction.

Our experience of our first ten years of urodynamic evaluation of some 10 000 patients was recorded in 'The Little Red Book' (1979 Urol. Clin. N. Amer. **6**.). Within this time, we reviewed the urodynamic significance of many traditional concepts that did not seem to 'hold water' and developed the standard intravenous urogram (IVU) into the urodynamically-more-meaningful intravenous urodynamogram (IVUD)—and the ultrasound cystodynamogram (USCD).

Over the last ten years the importance of objective functional evaluation to the success of surgical procedures that are designed to resolve urinary trace dysfunction has gradually become widely recognised—this is reflected in a great increase in the proportion of urodynamically-verified contributions to general urological meetings and in the establishment of many urodynamic referral clinics throughout the UK and most European countries.

However it has to be said that a simple survey of the level of patient satisfaction after common surgical procedures for the resolution of functional disorders—such as prostatic obstruction and female urinary incontinence—is still nowhere near as high as it should be and this has to be largely because many patients are allowed—or even encouraged—to have unrealistic expectations: this in turn must reflect either a lack of urodynamic insight on the part of some surgeons—or their failure to communicate it to their patients.

Thus, for instance, failure to recognise that the symptoms of frequency, urgency and nocturia are most commonly the result of unstable detrusor behaviour—and that some 20% of males over the age of 65–70 suffer this on an age-related basis in the *absence* of bladder outlet obstruction—is still a common source of misconception. It means that 20% of men with proven outlet obstruction are likely to be disappointed by the persistence of these symptoms after their prostatic resection if this fact has not been properly explained to them—otherwise they naturally assume that they will disappear. Inevitably almost all patients are dissatisfied if they have had a resection—or a *re-resection*—for *non-obstructive instability* because an erroneous diagnosis of outlet obstruction was based on their symptoms without urodynamically-acceptable verification.

Unfortunately such things still happen—worldwide. If simple uroflowmetry is not routinely used for the investigation of every patient attending a urological clinic with voiding symptoms, prostatic obstruction will be over-diagnosed, dyssynergic bladder neck obstruction will be under-diagnosed—and surgeons will tend to over-estimate their prowess at transurethral resection. It has to be questionable whether surgeons who do not routinely use uroflowmetry should advise and practice obstruction-relieving operations—the clinical situation is almost comparable to that of treating hypertension without using a sphygmomanometer.

For this and for many other reasons there is indeed a great need for this book—to explain, simply, what 'urodynamics' is all about to *all clinicians* whose patients have disorders of urinary tract function. Urodynamic insight is essential, not only for understanding and for successful surgical restoration of function, but also for appropriate patient communication. Hence Christopher and Tim have written it not just for urologists, but for surgeons, physicians, radiologists, general practitioners, students and senior nurses—all of these—and more.

1990                                                          R. T.-W.

*Dedication*

*To R. T.-W., C. P. B., G. W. and M. R. C., without whom none of this would have been possible*

# Preface

It is a much quoted, yet often ignored, adage that 'the bladder is an unreliable witness'. The refinement of urodynamic techniques, coupled with the rapid advancement in available electronic equipment which has occurred in the last 20 years, has allowed the widespread application of objective investigations to assist in the clarification of urinary tract symptoms. It is the intention of this guide to the subject to review the principles and practice of urodynamics as applied to the routine clinical management of patients.

The term *urodynamics* refers to the study of pressure and flow relationships relating to the storage and transport of urine within the urinary tract. In routine practice the majority of urodynamic investigative techniques carried out are centred on the lower urinary tract—investigating bladder filling and voiding function, thereby allowing the accurate definition of disorders of bladder storage and an assessment of the degree of voiding dysfunction. Upper tract urodynamics is uncommon outside specialist units.

Although the term urodynamics appears guaranteed in many quarters to inspire images of mysticism and of an esoteric subject requiring complex equipment, which is of limited applicability and best confined to the 'ivory towers', nothing could be further from the truth. Indeed, the basic principles involved in urodynamics are simple and in the majority of cases complex investigation is unnecessary. Certain factors have tended to foster this popular image.

Firstly, the application of theoretical physics to the subject, whilst producing useful models from which to base further research, is of limited usefulness to the practising clinician. It is, however, useful to consider the urinary tract as a series of conduits within which the movement of urine is dictated by the pressures acting upon it and the resistance to flow produced by the conduits through which it passes, with specific sphincteric mechanisms acting as zones of variable resistance. Secondly, jargon terms have tended to complicate and obscure otherwise logical and straightforward concepts. In order to clarify this as far as possible, the official terminology and units relating to urodynamics (presented in the format specified by the International Continence Society) are reviewed in depth in the text.

London 1990.                                                                                      C.R.C.
                                                                                                  T.J.C.

*Acknowledgement*

We would like to thank the International Continence Society for permission to use figures and definitions from their standardisation document.

# Contents

# 1. What urodynamics investigates —anatomy, innervation and function of the lower urinary tract

The urinary tract consists of two mutually dependent components: upper tract—kidneys and ureters and lower tract—bladder and urethra. This provides a highly sophisticated system of conduits, which allows the conversion of a continuous involuntary production of urine by the kidneys into the intermittent, consciously controlled voiding of urine (micturition) in appropriate circumstances. The upper tracts function as a low pressure distensible conduit with intrinsic peristalsis which transports urine from the nephrons via the ureters to the bladder. The vesicoureteric mechanism protects the nephrons from damage by the retrograde transmission of back pressure or infection from the bladder. The urinary bladder fulfils two main functions, the collection and low pressure storage of urine and its subsequent expulsion at an appropriate time and place.

## BLADDER STRUCTURE AND INNERVATION

The human bladder has three histological layers: an outer adventitial connective tissue layer, a middle smooth muscle coat (detrusor muscle), comprising a functional syncytium of interlacing muscle bundles, and an innermost lining comprised of transitional cell epithelium, providing an elastic barrier impervious to urine (Fig. 1.1). The detrusor muscle is under the control of the autonomic nervous system and receives a rich innervation from three groups of nerves. The principal population is comprised of presumptive cholinergic

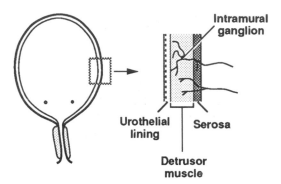

**Fig. 1.1** Structure of the bladder wall. The bladder wall is comprised of three layers and receives a rich innervation comprising cholinergic, adrenergic and non-adrenergic, non-cholinergic sensorimotor nerves. There are a number of intramural ganglia allowing extensive neural interaction to occur.

nerves, identified by their content of the enzyme acetylcholinesterase and demonstrated by the use of electron microscopy to lie in close apposition to muscle cells. Acting via the release of the neurotransmitter acetylcholine, these provide the major motor control of the detrusor muscle. In contrast, the sympathetic innervation comprises a sparse distribution of noradrenergic neurones, which occur in greatest concentration towards the bladder base and are thought to be of principal importance in the control of vasculature. Nevertheless, the close juxtaposition of these two neural populations raise the potential for functional interaction between the parasympathetic and sympathetic nervous systems. The third population of nonadrenergic noncholinergic (NANC) sensorimotor nerves contain a number of putative neurotransmitters (principally peptides), which can be identified by the use of immunofluorescent techniques. The role of the NANC innervation of the human bladder is as yet poorly understood.

The spinal segments S2-S4 acting via efferent parasympathetic cholinergic neurons are responsible for the initiation and maintenance of detrusor contraction. Damage to these spinal segments results in

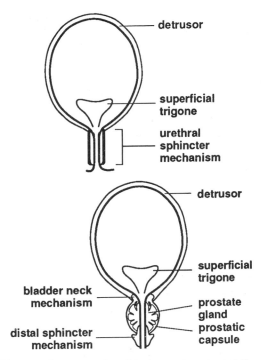

**Fig. 1.2** Diagrammatic representation of the lower urinary tract. **A** Female. **B** Male.

abolition of the micturition reflex in humans. After leaving the sacral foramina, the pelvic splanchnic nerves containing the parasympathetic innervation to the bladder pass lateral to the rectum to enter the inferior hypogastric or pelvic plexus. They are joined by the hypogastric nerve containing efferent sympathetic nerve fibres originating from the lower three thoracic and upper two lumbar segments of the spinal cord. When combined they form a plexus lying at the base of the bladder. It has been suggested that the main afferent pathway of the micturition reflex is via the pelvic nerves, with additional afferent information transmitted from the trigone via sympathetic neuronal pathways in the hypogastric nerves and some bladder and urethral sensation via the spinothalamic tracts.

## SPHINCTERIC MECHANISMS

Apart from the obvious anatomical differences relating to the longer urethra and presence of a prostate gland in the male, there are important differences between the two sexes relating to the histological structure, innervation and function of the outflow tract. In the male there are two important sphincteric mechanisms, a proximal 'bladder neck mechanism' and a urethral sphincteric mechanism lying at the apex of the prostate (the 'distal sphincter mechanism'). It must be remembered that the male bladder neck is a powerful sphincter, not only of the urinary, but also of the genital tract, the latter function being of primary importance in the prevention of retrograde ejaculation. The distal sphincteric mechanism is also extremely important as evidenced by its ability to maintain continence even when the bladder neck has been rendered totally incompetent by bladder neck incision or prostatectomy. In comparison, the female bladder neck is a far weaker structure and, indeed, even in nulliparous young women, can be incompetent (Fig. 1.2). Urinary continence in women therefore usually relies upon the integrity of the intrinsic urethral sphincteric mechanism—damage to the innervation of the urethral sphincter by obstetric trauma predisposes to urinary stress incontinence.

These functional observations are mirrored by the ultrastructural findings. The male bladder neck consists of two muscular layers, a powerful inner layer of muscle bundles orientated in a circular fashion and containing a rich adrenergic sympathetic nerve supply, and an outer layer contiguous with the detrusor muscle and receiving a similar innervation. In contrast, the female bladder neck is poorly defined, with the principal orientation of muscle fibres being in a longitudinal direction and the predominant innervation being cholinergic. The urethral sphincter mechanism is composed of intrinsic urethral smooth muscle and extrinsic striated muscle

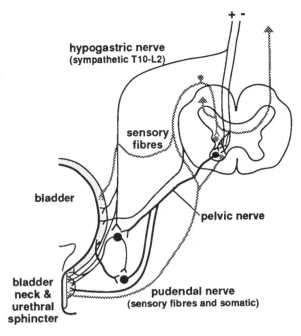

**Fig. 1.3** Diagrammatic representation of the neural control of the lower urinary tract. It is important to recognise that there is extensive interaction both within the spinal cord and in paravesical pelvic ganglia and intramural bladder ganglia (not shown).

components. In the female it extends throughout the proximal two-thirds of the urethra, whilst in the male the distal sphincter mechanism is localised to the prostatic apex. Although urethral smooth muscle receives a dual autonomic innervation, the sympathetic nervous system predominates in the male and the parasympathetic in the female (Fig. 1.3).

The efferent innervation of the striated muscle of the extrinsic component of the urethral sphincter arises predominantly from cell bodies lying in a specific area of the sacral anterior horn known as Onuf's nucleus. A number of aspects of the innervation of this sphincter are still controversial, with regard not only to the neural pathways involved, but also the relative contribution of somatic and autonomic nerves. The limited knowledge available suggests that the pudendal nerve transmits urethral mucosal sensation.

## MECHANISMS OF URINE STORAGE AND MICTURITION

### Reflexes governing micturition

Before considering the clinical investigation and treatment of disorders of micturition, it is first essential to consider the neural mechanisms controlling urinary tract function. Most of the contemporary knowledge is based on studies with experimental animals. Although it is very difficult and, indeed, often misleading to relate the findings of such animal models directly to man, such information is essential since only limited data are available on humans as they can only be obtained from the study of clearly defined clinical syndromes and isolated spinal cord lesions.

Barrington initially described five reflexes associated with micturition in the cat, to which he added a further two on the basis of further study. Two of these reflexes had their reflex centres in supraspinal sites (medulla and pons) and caused strong and sustained contractions. He considered these as essential for normal micturition, since bladder contraction and urethral relaxation were not coordinated after experimentally produced high spinal transection. The remaining five reflexes appeared confined to the spinal cord. More recently it has been proposed that many interrelated reflexes act upon the sacral micturition centre, exerting both excitatory and inhibitory effects.

Lower urinary tract function includes two interrelated yet distinct phases, urine storage and voiding; these will now be considered in more detail.

### Urine storage

The bladder and urethra, by virtue of the muscle and connective tissue which they contain, possess intrinsic tone. At rest, this urethral tone keeps the walls in apposition and positively aids continence. During filling, the walls of the bladder exhibit receptive relaxation, i.e. the ability of the vesical lumen to expand without a concomitant rise in intravesical pressure. The extent to which a change in volume ($\delta V$) occurs as related to a change in intravesical pressure ($\delta P$) is known as the bladder compliance ($\delta V/\delta P$). Factors which contribute to this property are the passive viscoelastic properties of the bladder and the intrinsic ability of smooth muscle to maintain a constant tension over a wide range of stretch. The other major factor controlling bladder filling is its neural control.

During bladder filling afferent activity from stretch receptors increases and passes via the posterior roots of the sacral cord and the lateral spinothalamic tracts to the brain, thereby mediating the desire to void. Activity within the striated component of the urethral sphincter is increased, local spinal reflex activity enhances the activity within striated muscles of the pelvic floor and sphincter.

Local factors are important during bladder filling and these include not only receptive relaxation, but also the passive viscoelastic properties of the bladder wall. Both abnormal bladder morphology resulting from collagenous infiltration, hypertrophy or altered muscle structure (e.g. obstructed bladder) and abnormal detrusor smooth muscle behaviour, either primary or secondary to neural dysfunction, could contribute to the genesis of poor bladder compliance and detrusor instability (vide infra).

## Initiation and control of voiding

Once a threshold level of filling has been achieved (which will depend on circumstances and vary between individuals), increasing afferent activity will start to impinge on consciousness and the subject will become aware that the bladder is filling up. Except during infancy, the normal human has complete volitional control over these reflex pathways. In appropriate circumstances voiding will be initiated. When micturition is initiated by the cerebral cortex a complex series of bladder/brain-stem reflexes are likely to be involved.

During voiding, urethral relaxation precedes detrusor contraction, there is a simultaneous relaxation of the pelvic floor muscles and these events are accompanied by funnelling of the bladder neck. The mechanism of these changes is poorly understood. It is likely that following increased activity within parasympathetic neurones, central inhibitory influences acting on sacral centres are removed and voiding is initiated under the influence of pontine medullary centres. This allows parasympathetically controlled detrusor contraction to occur, with a corresponding relaxation of the urethra/prostate/bladder neck complex resulting from reciprocal nerve-mediated inhibition. In addition to these primary actions, other important secondary events are: 1. contraction of the diaphragm and anterior abdominal wall muscles, 2. relaxation of the pelvic floor, and 3. the specific behavioural changes associated with voiding.

At the end of voiding, the proximal urethra is closed in a retrograde fashion, the 'milkback' seen at videocystometry. Once these events are completed, inhibition is reapplied to the sacral centres by the cortex and the next filling cycle restarts.

## Normal vesicourethral function

The normal function of the human lower urinary tract is dependent upon integrated co-ordination of the neural control of both the bladder and outflow tract, for which an intact spinal cord is essential. Under normal circumstances the bladder capacity is approximately 500 ml and the bladder empties leaving no residue. The male voids at a pressure of $40-50$ cm $H_2O$ and a maximum flow rate of $30-40$ ml/s, whilst the female voids at a pressure of $30-40$ cm $H_2O$ and a maximum flow rate of $40-50$ ml/s; the sex difference can be related to the higher outflow resistance exerted by the male urethra.

## Abnormal vesicourethral function

Disordered lower urinary tract function may follow disruption of the normal peripheral or central nervous system control mechanisms or may result from disordered bladder muscle function, either primary (of unknown aetiology), or secondary to an identifiable pathology, such as prostatic outflow obstruction.

Although many of the disorders seen in clinical practice may well have an underlying neurological basis, a classification based on specific abnormalities and in particular the site of a neurological lesion is not practical for the following reasons; the aetiology and pathogenesis of many disorders is at present unclear, lesions are often difficult to locate specifically and, indeed, once located can be difficult to relate to the neurological signs (c.f. multiple sclerosis) and different lesions may produce identical functional changes in the lower urinary tract. Nevertheless, a neurological classification is invaluable for counselling purposes and can be of useful prognostic significance; certain characteristic patterns can be identified.

*1. Peripheral denervation.* The clinical picture is dependent upon the extent of denervation. Complete lesions decentralise the lower urinary tract and, although ganglionic activity may persist, an acontractile bladder will result, with an inactive urethra. Subsequent continence will be governed by the degree of continence of the bladder neck mechanism. The urethra will have a fixed resistance and the efficiency of bladder emptying will be dependent on abdominal straining or manual compression.

*2. Suprasacral spinal cord lesions.* If the spinal cord is transected above the fifth lumbar segment, the state of 'cord bladder' develops. A principal feature of this lesion is the loss of co-ordinated detrusor sphincter behaviour, which results in synchronous contraction of the detrusor and urethral sphincter (detrusor sphincter dyssynergia). Sphincter contractions are not usually prolonged throughout the period of detrusor action and hence some voiding does occur, but there is considerable retention of urine. In a number of patients with lesions of the thoracolumbar cord, voiding function is particularly ineffective and in these low compliance is an important feature.

**3. Cerebral (suprapontine lesions).** Lesions of the midbrain rarely result in disturbances of continence and micturition. It is likely that this is a consequence partly of the bilateral representation of nuclei at this level and partly of the poor prognosis of patients with extensive lesions. Damage to the basal ganglia results in a reduced threshold for the transmission of impulses through the reticulospinal tracts controlling micturition; hence the typical picture of involuntary bladder contractions seen in patients with Parkinson's disease and following cerebrovascular accidents. Lesions of the cerebral cortex, in particular involving the inner surface of the cerebral hemispheres or the frontal cortex, can result in incontinence.

The majority of patients encountered in routine clinical practice represent a heterogenous collection for whom no identifiable neurological abnormality is at present apparent. No doubt a number of these patients nevertheless have an, as yet, unidentified neural disorder (c.f. primary idiopathic detrusor instability, as contrasted to postobstructive secondary detrusor instability, where a peripheral disruption of local neuromuscular control is likely to be a major aetiological factor).

# 2. Investigation of urinary function—urodynamic techniques

Urinary continence during bladder filling, urine storage in the bladder and the efficiency of subsequent voiding all depend on the accurate co-ordination of the opposing forces of detrusor contraction and the urethral closure pressure. Symptomatic evaluation of urinary tract dysfunction is difficult, since the bladder often proves to be an 'unreliable witness', not only because of subjective bias, but also because there is considerable overlap between symptom complexes. Investigation of lower urinary tract function uses the scientific principles of urodynamics, the techniques for which were first refined at the Middlesex Hospital.

Whilst the interpretation of urodynamics can, of course, be complex on occasion, in the majority of cases the indications for urodynamic investigation are evident and its application provides an essential complement to the modern practice of urology, gynaecology and associated specialties. Although it is tempting to use other terms for the disorders one encounters when practising urodynamic investigation, it is essential to standardise the jargon used in order to allow the accurate exchange and comparison of information for both clinical and experimental purposes. Therefore, the official terminology suggested by the International Continence Society is reviewed below.

Urodynamics encompasses a number of complimentary techniques of varying degrees of complexity, the application of which needs to be tailored to meet the clinical requirements of each case. These techniques are:

*Simple urodynamics*

1. Volume voided charts
2. Pad testing
3. Flow rate
4. Ultrasound cystodynamogram
5. Intravenous urodynamogram
6. Cystometry
7. Videocystometrography

*Complex urodynamics*

1. Urethral pressure measurement
2. Neurophysiological investigation
3. Upper tract urodynamics (the Whitaker test).

## VOLUME VOIDED CHARTS

The urodynamic value of the simple voiding chart is often overlooked—an important omission since this is a natural volumetric urodynamic record of bladder function. A normal bladder fills to a capacity approximating to its functional capacity and the chart records a series of sizeable ( > 500 ml) and fairly consistent volumes. An unstable bladder contracts at variable degrees of distension before full capacity, erroneously informing the patient that it is full.

### Technique

The patient is instructed to *hold-on* up to maximum capacity before each voiding over a consecutive period of 48 hours, to measure the volume of each void accurately and to record it on a chart.

### Practical guidelines

In sensory frequency resulting from hypersensitive bladder states due to urine infection, trigonitis, etc. the symptoms and voided chart often vary considerably from week to week.

It is essential not to base therapy on the results of such investigation alone; in particular, it is essential to exclude a sinister aetiology for bladder symptoms, such as neoplasia, stone, etc. before proceeding with therapy.

## Comment

The voided volume chart may provide information that is helpful in both the assessment and treatment of bladder dysfunction. It is particularly useful in providing a form of biofeedback during bladder retraining. It is important, however, not to overinterpret the results obtained, but to use them in combination with other forms of urodynamic and urological assessment.

## PAD TESTING

### The quantification of urine loss

The subjective assessment of incontinence is often difficult to interpret and may not indicate reliably the degree of abnormality. In order to obtain a representative result, especially in subjects with variable or intermittent urinary incontinence, the test should occupy as long a period as possible, in circumstances which should approximate to those of everyday life; yet be as practical as possible in the available circumstances and be carried out in a standardised fashion.

### Technique

On the basis of pilot studies performed in various centres, the ICS has suggested a number of guidelines which are repeated verbatim here.

It is recommended that the test should occupy a 1-hour period during which a series of standard activities are carried out. This test *can* be extended by further 1-hour periods if the result of the first 1-hour test was not considered representative by either the patient or the investigator. Alternatively, the test can be repeated having filled the bladder to a defined volume.

The total amount of urine lost during the test period is determined by weighing a collecting device, such as a nappy, absorbent pad or condom appliance. A nappy or pad should be worn inside waterproof underpants or should have a waterproof backing. Care should be taken to use a collecting device of adequate capacity.

Immediately before the test begins, the collecting device is weighed to the nearest gram.

## Typical test schedule

1. Test is started without the patient voiding.

2. Preweighed collecting device is put on and first 1-hour test period begins.

3. Subject drinks 500 ml sodium-free liquid within a short period (maximum 15 mins), then sits or rests.

4. Half-hour period: subject walks, including climbing equivalent to one flight up and down.

5. During the remaining period the subject performs the following activities:

   (i)   standing up from sitting, 10 times
   (ii)  coughing vigorously, 10 times
   (iii) running on the spot for 1 minute
   (iv) bending to pick up small object from floor, 5 times
   (v)  wash hands in running water for 1 minute

6. At the end of the 1-hour test the collecting device is removed and weighed.

7. If the test is regarded as representative, the subject voids and the volume is recorded.

8. Otherwise the test is repeated, preferably without voiding.

## Practical guidelines

### Weight of urine

If the collecting device becomes saturated or filled during the test, it should be removed and weighed, and replaced by a fresh device.

The total weight of urine lost during the test period is taken to be equal to the gain in weight of the collecting device(s).

*Interpretation*

In interpreting the results of the test it should be borne in mind that a weight gain of up to 1 gram may be due to weighing errors, sweating or vaginal discharge.

The activity programmed may be modified according to the subject's physical ability.

*Variations*

If substantial variations from the usual test schedule occur, this should be recorded so that the same schedule can be used on subsequent occasions.

In some situations the timing of the test (e.g. in relation to the menstrual cycle) may be relevant.

*Voiding*

In principle the subject should not void during the test period. If the patient experiences urgency, then he/she should be persuaded to postpone voiding and to perform as many of the activities in section 5 as possible in order to detect leakage. Before voiding the collection device is removed for weighing. If inevitable voiding cannot be postponed, then the test is terminated. The voiding volume and the duration of the test should be recorded. For subjects not completing the full test the results may require separate analysis, or the test may be repeated after rehydration.

The test result is given as grams of urine lost in the 1-hour test period in which the greatest urine loss is recorded.

Additional procedures intended to give information of diagnostic value are permissible provided they do not interfere with the basic test. For example, additional changes and weighing of the collecting device can give information about the timing of urine loss. The absorbent nappy may be an electronic recording nappy so that the timing is recorded directly.

## Comment

This type of study is easy to conduct and interpret and provides a great deal of useful information. The weight of the urine lost during the test is measured and recorded in grams. A loss of less than one gram is within experimental error and the patients should be regarded as essentially dry.

## FLOW RATE

The simplest and often most useful investigation in the assessment of voiding dysfunction is the measurement of urinary flow rate. On the basis of this test it is often possible objectively to confirm the presence of bladder outlet obstruction. Studies have demonstrated that simple uroflowmetry by itself is adequate investigation for uncomplicated prostate outflow obstruction in nearly 50% of patients. In a number of instances, for example where a result is obtained which is at variance with the patient's symptoms or where symptoms remain despite surgical correction, more detailed investigation is indicated. In addition, it must be remembered that a normal flow rate can be present in the early stages of obstruction as a consequence of a compensatory increase in voiding pressure which allows the maintenance of an apparently normal flow rate.

## Technique

The flow rate is measured with a flow meter, which is a device that measures and indicates a quantity of fluid (volume or mass) passed per unit time; such machines normally indicate the volumetric flow rate. The measurement is expressed in ml/s. The commonly used flow meters employ the following methods.

### 1. Rotating disc method

The voided fluid is directed onto a rotating disc. The amount landing on the disc produces a proportionate increase in its inertia and the power required to keep the disc rotating at a constant rate is measured, thereby allowing calculation of the flow rate of fluid past the disc.

### 2. Electronic dipstick method

A dipstick is mounted in a collecting chamber and as urine accumulates the electrical capacitance of the dipstick changes. This allows calculation of the rate of accumulation of fluid and hence the flow rate.

### 3. Gravimetric method

Such instruments measure the weight of collected fluid or the hydrostatic pressure at the base of a collecting cylinder. This similarly allows calculation of a flow rate. A flow rate estimation can be carried out either by itself or in combination with other techniques (USCD, IVUD, CMG, VCMG).

## Practical guidelines

The important factors to consider when interpreting a flow rate are the *rate* and *pattern* (in particular whether the flow is *continuous* or *intermittent*). A number of characteristic traces are shown in Figure 2.1. In carrying out a urinary flow rate estimation, particular attention needs to be paid to certain factors which can influence the result obtained.

1. Voided volumes of less than 150–200 ml can lead to erroneous results.

2. If possible, the patient should be in favourable surroundings and should not be stressed unduly.

3. Whether the patient is voiding supine or standing.

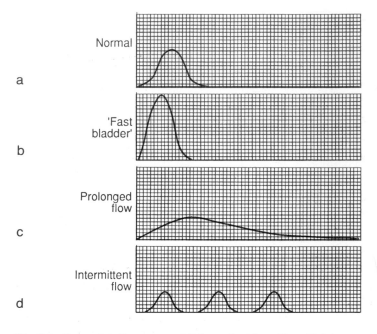

**Fig. 2.1**   Characteristic flow patterns of (a) 'normal' voiding with rapid change before and after the peak flow, (b) 'fast bladder' trace representing an exaggeration of normal; associated with the high end filling pressure seen in cases of detrusor instability, (c) 'prolonged flow' associated with relative outflow obstruction, (d) 'intermittent flow' resulting from abdominal straining superimposed on poor detrusor function.

4. Whether the flow rate is a so called 'free flow rate' occurring after natural filling, or is in the presence of a bladder-filling catheter.

## Definitions

*Voided volume.* The total volume expelled via the urethra.
*Maximum flow rate.* The maximum measured value of the flow rate.

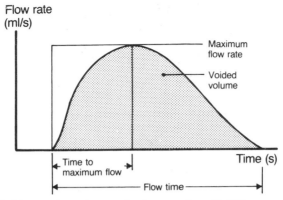

**Fig. 2.2**  Diagram of a continuous urine flow recording with ICS recommended nomenclature. (Reproduced with permission from the Scandinavian Journal of Urology and Nephrology, 114, 1988.)

*Average flow rate.* Voided volume divided by flow time. The calculation of average flow rate is only meaningful if flow is continuous and without terminal dribbling.

*Flow time.* The time over which measurable flow actually occurs.

*Time to maximum flow.* The elapsed time from onset of flow to maximum flow. The flow pattern must be described when flow time and average flow rate are measured.

*Intermittent flow.* The same parameters used to characterise continuous flow may be applicable if care is exercised in patient with intermittent flow. In measuring flow time the time intervals between flow episodes are disregarded.

*Voiding time.* Total duration of micturition, ie, including interruptions. When voiding is completed without interruption, voiding time is equal to flow time (Fig. 2.2).

## Comment

It is evident that the urinary flow rate provides important and useful information suggesting whether there is obstruction to the outflow tract. Perusal of the flow rate pattern may indicate a possible aetiology.

*Drawbacks*

The flow rate can be misleading:

1. If there has been detrusor compensation, for example, the flow rate is maintained at fairly normal values due to high voiding detrusor pressures.

2. The flow rate is not diminished until the urethral calibre is reduced below 11 Ch.

3. The flow rate may be misleading in patients where there is significant detrusor decompensation leaving large residuals.

4. The flow rate can be influenced by straining and this should be taken into account when interpreting results.

5. Irregularities in the measured flow rate can be due to collecting funnel artefacts and to variations in the direction of the urinary stream.

Uroflowmetry by itself is an adequate investigation for uncomplicated prostate outflow obstruction in nearly 50% of patients. It is also invaluable in the assessment of voiding function across a spectrum of urological conditions. It must, however, be emphasised that most reliance should be placed on the observed flow pattern rather than an undue weight being given to absolute values obtained. In view of the limitations outlined above, in certain circumstances where doubt remains following a flow rate, or in particular where previous surgery has been carried out, more complex investigations are required. To provide more detailed information a simple flow rate can be combined with X-ray or ultrasound imaging.

## ULTRASOUND CYSTODYNAMOGRAM (USCD)

Ultrasound is combined with a flow rate to provide more detailed information on bladder function (Fig. 2.3).

### Technique

The full bladder is scanned, the patient voids into a flow meter in private and a postvoiding scan is carried out to assess bladder

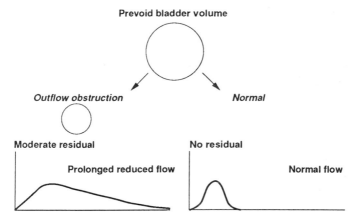

**Fig. 2.3** The ultrasound cystodynamogram.

residual. Interpretation of the flow rate takes account of the factors mentioned above. Any form of ultrasound probe allowing adequate visualisation of the bladder is used. The patient should be scanned at the time that they feel 'full', thereby providing an idea of the functional bladder capacity. Similarly, the patient should be scanned as soon after voiding as possible in order to provide accurate assessment of the true bladder residual.

## Practical guidelines

1. Ensure that the patient has a subjectively full bladder prior to carrying out the study to provide a representative result.

2. Make sure that the study is carried out in circumstances where the patient is relaxed, so as not to introduce error into the results obtained.

### Comment

The USCD provides data on bladder capacity of the flow rate and postvoiding residual, producing a more detailed assessment of the lower urinary tract function than a flow rate alone. It can be carried out quickly and easily with little specialised equipment, is non-invasive and does not use ionising radiation. It is of particular value in the follow up of patients attending clinics. For instance, with a hypocontractile detrusor following surgery for the relief of obstruction or, where it is suspected that voiding efficiency may have been compromised, eg after a repair procedure for stress incontinence.

## INTRAVENOUS URODYNAMOGRAM (IVUD).

The intravenous urodynamogram (IVUD) provides significantly more information than the conventional intravenous urogram by virtue of its combination with a free flow rate. (Fig 2.4.)

### Technique

In addition to the appropriate upper tract films of an intravenous urogram it includes a voiding flow rate carried out when the patient feels the bladder to be naturally full (an event which can be hastened by the use of a suitable diuretic). The subsequent post-micturition film after natural micturition allows accurate assessment of the patient's true bladder residual volume.

### Practical guidelines

As for ultrasound cystodynamogram

### Comment

In many patients with outflow obstruction this provides a sufficiently comprehensive assessment upon which to base further treatment. It is of particular value since this test can easily be integrated into the routine of the radiology department and involves little additional equipment or staff training.

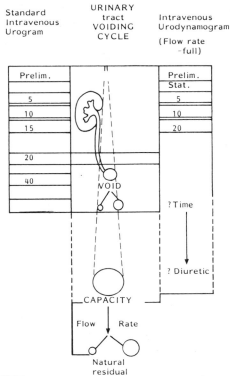

**Fig. 2.4**  The IVUD.

## CYSTOMETRY AND VIDEOCYSTOMETROGRAPHY

### Which test—cystometry or videocystometrography?

The majority of urodynamic units do not have the benefit of fluoroscopic screening or video recording facilities. In the assessment of the majority of patients presenting with urinary frequency and urgency simple cystometry provides all of the necessary information. Synchronous cystography and cystometry recordings (VCMG) are most important in the assessment of complex cases, particularly where previous surgery has failed; since this investigation allows a combined anatomical and functional evaluation of lower urinary tract function. Nevertheless, it must be remembered that simple cystourethrography can be carried out in all X-ray departments. A point worth remembering in the investigation of simple stress incontinence without urinary frequency or urgency where the stress incontinence is not clinically demonstrable, is that a cough test carried out during cystography alone may be all that is required to confirm the diagnosis prior to surgical correction.

## Cystometry

In equivocal or more complex cases, detailed urodynamic investigation is necessary. *Cystometry* is the method by which the pressure/volume relationship of the bladder is measured. The term *cystometry* is usually taken to mean the measurement of detrusor pressure during controlled bladder filling and subsequent voiding with measurement of the synchronous flow rate (filling and voiding cystometry). Cystometry is used to assess detrusor activity, sensation, capacity and compliance.

## VIDEOCYSTOMETROGRAPHY
*(video = I see; cystometry + cystourethrography)*

If appropriate radiological facilities exist, the bladder can be filled with contrast media, thus allowing the simultaneous screening of the bladder and outflow tract during filling and voiding to be conducted (cystourethrography). When these two procedures are combined, this results in the gold standard investigation: the videocystometrogram (Fig. 2.5A).

Radiological screening provides valuable additional anatomical information on the appearances of the bladder, the presence of ureteric reflux, the level of any outflow obstruction in the lower urinary tract, the degree of support to the bladder base during coughing and, by itself, is more than adequate for the diagnosis of sphincteric competence. This information, along with the

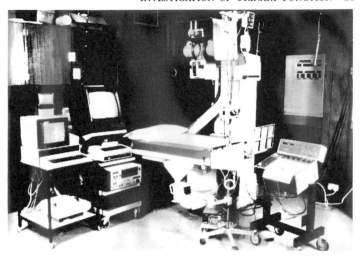

**Fig. 2.5 A** Videocystometrography suite.

accompanying pressure flow traces, can be recorded on a video tape allowing subsequent review and discussion. The majority of patients can be investigated adequately using the simpler urodynamic techniques described, including simple cystometry. Videocystometry is, however, essential for the adequate assessment of the complex cases where equivocal results have been obtained from simpler investigations for the definition of neuropathic disorders, and in situations where there has been an apparent failure of a previous surgical procedure.

## Technique for videocystometrography/cystometry

The detrusor pressure is estimated by the automatic subtraction of rectal pressure (as an index of intra-abdominal pressure) from the total bladder pressure, thus removing the influence of artefacts produced by abdominal straining. During this study, notice is taken of the initial bladder residual, the bladder volume at the time of the patient's first sensation of filling. the final tolerated bladder volume and the final residual volume after voiding. All systems are zeroed at

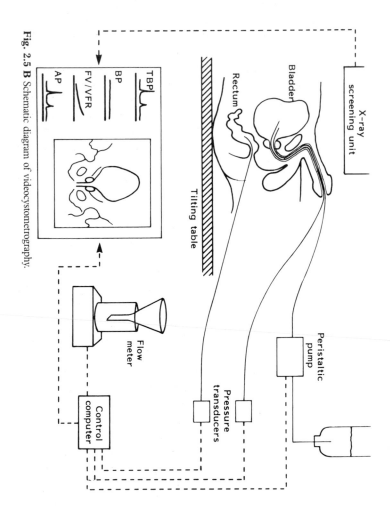

**Fig. 2.5 B** Schematic diagram of videocystometrography.

atmospheric pressure. For external transducers, the reference point is the level of the superior edge of the symphysis pubis. For catheter mounted transducer the reference point is the transducer itself.

Patients, excluding those with indwelling catheters, are asked to void into a flowmeter to allow measurement of a free flow rate. They are then requested to lie in the left lateral position on an X-ray screening table whilst a 2 mm diameter saline-filled catheter is introduced into the rectum, the end of the tube being protected with a finger stall to prevent faecal blockage (a slit is cut in this to prevent tamponade producing artefactual results during the study). With the patient in the supine position, the external urethral meatus is cleaned with antiseptic solution. The urethra is anaesthetised with 1% lignocaine gel containing chlorohexidine. A 10 Ch Nelaton filling catheter with a 1 mm diameter saline-filled plastic pressure catheter inserted into the subterminal side hole is gently inserted into the bladder and the two catheters then disengaged. The bladder is drained of urine and this initial residual volume recorded.

The principles of the technique used are demonstrated on the accompanying schematic diagram (Fig 2.5B).

The two pressure measurement lines are then connected to the transducers incorporated in the urodynamic apparatus. The lines are flushed through with saline, great care being taken to exclude all air bubbles from both the tubing and transducer chambers. Contrast medium at room temperature is then instilled into the bladder at a predetermined rate under the control a peristaltic pump. Fast-fill (> 100 ml/min) is used routinely in our unit, although slower filling rates approaching the physiological range are mandatory in the assessment of the neuropathic bladder.

The bladder is filled initially in the supine position and the volume at first sensation of filling is noted. When the subject first experiences discomfort, the radiographic table is tipped towards the standing position and subsequent bladder filling discontinued when at the maximum tolerated capacity. During bladder filling the patient is asked to consciously suppress bladder contraction. The Nelaton filling catheter is then removed from the bladder and the patient turned to the oblique position relative to the X-ray machine and asked to void into the flowmeter provided.

Throughout the study continuous rectal pressure, total bladder pressure and electronically subtracted detrusor pressure (total bladder pressure minus rectal pressure) measurements are sampled at a predetermined rate (1 Hz on most commercially available contemporary machines) and the results displayed on the video display unit/stored to disc/polygraph chart recorder—depending on the equipment in use.

The adjacent X-ray screening apparatus allows the synchronous display of pressure and flow, and also radiographic data relating to bladder morphology, ureteric reflux and the appearances of the bladder outlet and urethra, to be displayed alongside the numerical data on a video display unit. The monitor images are recorded on video tape allowing review and detailed study.

## Practical points

A number of variations in technique are currently available and the following points deserve specific consideration.

### Access

Whilst the majority of cystometry is carried out via the transurethral route, percutaneous placement of catheters both for bladder filling and pressure measurement is essential in the investigation of paediatric patients.

### Type of catheter

1. Fluid-filled catheter—specify number of catheters, single or multiple lumens, type of catheter, size of catheter.

2. Catheter tip transducer—specifications vary between manufacturers; these catheters tend to be expensive and rather too fragile for routine use.

*Measuring equipment*

A number of commercial urodynamic systems are currently available. These vary greatly in terms of sampling rate, associated computer software backup and price.

*Test medium (liquid or gas)*

This is obviously not applicable to catheter tip transducers. The advantage of equipment using gas as a medium is that it can be more compact and is therefore more easily portable. A major drawback with gas cystometry—*aerodynamics!*—is its susceptibility to artefact being introduced by changes in the temperature of the gaseous medium; a far less important consideration when fluid is used.

*Position of patient*

e.g. Supine, sitting or standing.

*Type of filling*

This may be by diuresis or catheter. Filling by catheter may be *continuous* or *incremental*; the precise filling rate should be stated (vide infra). When the incremental method is used the volume increment should be stated.

*Continuous or intermittent pressure measurement*

Continuous pressure measurement is of greatest usefulness in clinical practice. In patients, for example, where a suprapubic catheter is in place and where a urethral pressure line cannot be introduced per urethram. Alternate incremental filling of the bladder and cystometry can be carried out using the same catheter.

**Comment**

1. Before starting to fill the bladder the residual urine may be measured. However, the removal of a large volume of residual urine may alter detrusor function, especially in the neuropathic disorders.

Certain cystometric parameters may be significantly altered by the speed of bladder filling.

2. During cystometry it is taken for granted that the patient is awake, unanaesthetised and neither sedated, nor taking drugs that affect bladder function. Any variations from this ideal must be taken into account when interpreting results.

3. In a substantial number of women who present with incontinence, urinary leakage cannot be demonstrated either clinically or radiologically. Monitoring by an assessment of the amount of leakage into pads can be particularly helpful in this situation. Similarly, in a small group of patients complaining of significant symptoms, where no urodynamic abnormality is demonstrable on conventional testing, continuous ambulatory urodynamic monitoring is invaluable.

4. The failure of the bladder neck mechanism to relax occurs in a small percentage of young men resulting in a clinical entity of bladder neck obstruction (dyssynergia). This abnormality is evident during videocystometry if the patient is asked to inhibit micturition voluntarily. In a normal urodynamic study, contrast media will be milked back from the distal sphincter mechanism proximally through the bladder neck into the bladder, a normal *stop test*. If there is obstruction at the level of the bladder neck, contrast will be trapped within the prostatic urethra.

## Definitions

*Normal values*   During cystometry, under normal circumstances the bladder should fill to a capacity of approximately 500 ml before a strong desire to void is experienced. During subsequent bladder filling, whilst the patient is making a conscious effort to inhibit voiding, in practice the subtracted intravesical detrusor pressure should not rise significantly off its baseline value—although the International Continence Society no longer recognises a specific value as being essential to the diagnosis of detrusor instability. In practice, we have found that, if there is a pressure rise greater than

**Normal**

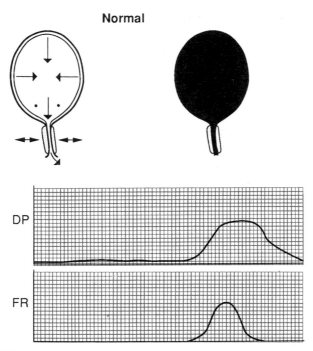

**Fig. 2.6** Normal videocystometrogram.

15 cm of water, then detrusor instability can be said to be present. The only exception is represented by a gradual linear rise in pressure during detrusor filling—so called *low compliance*—which, although clearly defined, remains an as yet poorly classified entity.

During subsequent voiding the patient's bladder empties completely with a maximum detrusor pressure of 30–50 cm of water and a maximum urinary flow rate of 30–40 ml/s in men and 40–50 ml/s in women.

***Compliance*** indicates the change in volume for a change in pressure. Compliance is calculated by dividing the volume change ($\delta V$) by the change in detrusor pressure ($\delta P_{det}$) during the change in bladder volume ($C = \delta V / \delta P_{det}$). Compliance is expressed as ml per cm $H_2O$.

## Filling rate

1. < 10 ml per minute is slow fill cystometry—'physiological filling'.
2. 10–100 ml per minute is medium fill cystometry
3. > 100 ml per minute is rapid fill cystometry.

## Bladder pressure measurements during filling

*Intravesical pressure* is the pressure within the bladder.

*Abdominal pressure* is taken to be the pressure surrounding the bladder. In current practice it is estimated from rectal or, less commonly, extraperitoneal pressure (Fig. 2.7).

*Detrusor pressure* is that component of intravesical pressure that is created by forces in the bladder wall (passive and active). It is estimated by subtracting abdominal pressure from intravesical pressure. The simultaneous measurement of abdominal pressure is essential for interpretation of the intravesical pressure trace. However, artefacts on the detrusor pressure trace may be produced by intrinsic rectal contractions.

*Bladder sensation*. Sensation is difficult to evaluate because of its subjective nature. It is usually assessed by questioning the patient in relation to the fullness of the bladder during cystometry.

### Definitions

Commonly used descriptive terms include:

*First desire to void*

*Normal desire to void* (this is defined as the feeling that leads the patient to pass urine at the next convenient moment, but voiding can be delayed if necessary).

*Strong desire to void* (this is defined as a persistent desire to void without the fear of leakage).

*Urgency* (this is defined as a strong desire to void accompanied by fear of leakage or fear of pain).

*Pain* (the site and character of which should be specified). Pain during bladder filling or micturition is abnormal.

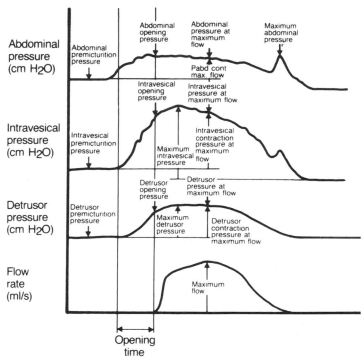

**Fig. 2.7** Diagram of a pressure flow recording of micturition with ICS recommended nomenclature. (Reproduced with permission from the Scandinavian Journal of Urology and Nephrology, 114, 1988.)

The term 'capacity' must be qualified:

***Maximum cystometric capacity***, in patients with normal sensation, is the volume at which the patient feels he/she can no longer delay micturition. In the absence of sensation the maximum cystometric capacity cannot be defined in the same terms and is the volume at which the clinician decided to terminate filling. In the presence of sphincter incompetence the maximum cystometric capacity may be significantly increased by occlusion of the urethra, e.g. by Foley catheter.

*Functional bladder capacity*, or voided volume, is more relevant and is assessed from a frequency/volume chart (urinary diary).

*Maximum (anaesthetic) bladder capacity* is the volume measured after filling during a deep general or spinal/epidural anaesthetic, at a specified fluid temperature, filling pressure and filling time.

## Bladder pressure measurements during micturition

*Opening time* is the elapsed time from initial rise in detrusor pressure to onset of flow. This is the initial isovolumetric contraction period of micturition. Time lags should be taken into account. In most urodynamic systems a time lag occurs equal to the time taken for the urine to pass from the point of pressure measurement to the uroflow transducer.

*Premicturition pressure* is the pressure recorded immediately before the initial isovolumetric contraction.

*Opening pressure* is the pressure recorded at the onset of measured flow.

*Maximum pressure* is the maximum value of the measured pressure.

*Pressure at maximum flow* is the pressure recorded at maximum measured flow rate.

*Contraction pressure at maximum flow* is the difference between pressure at maximum flow and premicturition pressure.

Postmicturition events (e.g. after contraction) are not well understood and so cannot be defined as yet.

*The Stop Test.* If this demonstrates the presence of contrast trapped in the posterior urethra, it may indicate bladder neck obstruction. Women, particularly those with stress incontinence are often unable to carry out a stop test.

*Isometric Pressure ($P_{ISO}$).* Detrusor pressure measured at the time of the stop test. The significance of the $P_{ISO}$ is controversial.

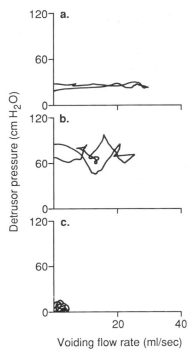

**Fig. 2.8** Pressure flow plots. (a) normal; (b) outflow obstruction; (c) low pressure/low flow.

## Pressure flow relationships

In the early days of urodynamics the flow rate and voiding pressure were related as a 'urethral resistance factor'. The concept of a resistance factor originates from rigid tube hydrodynamics. The urethra does not generally behave as a rigid tube as it is an irregular and distensible conduit whose walls and surroundings have active and passive elements and hence, influence the flow through it. Therefore, a resistance factor cannot provide a valid comparison between patients.

There are many ways of displaying the relationships between flow and pressure during micturition. As yet, available data do not permit a standard presentation of pressure/flow parameters. Figure 2.8

demonstrates a number of representative traces calculated by our software programme, demonstrating the relationship between pressure and flow parameters in a) an unobstructed urethra, b) an obstructed urethra, c) detrusor underactivity.

## Residual urine

Residual urine is defined as the volume of fluid remaining in the bladder immediately following the completion of micturition. The measurement of residual urine forms an integral part of the study of micturition. However, voiding in unfamiliar surroundings may lead to unrepresentative results, as may voiding on command with a partially filled or overfilled bladder. A number of the urodynamic studies discussed above measure the bladder residual volume. In each individual patient it is necessary to choose a method appropriate to the overall assessment of the clinical problem.

### *Important points in the interpretation of residual volume*

1. When estimating residual urine, the measurement of voided volume and the time interval between voiding and residual urine estimation should be recorded: this is particularly important if the patient is in a diuretic phase.

2. In the condition of vesicoureteric reflux, urine may re-enter the bladder after micturition and may falsely be interpreted as residual urine.

3. The presence of urine in bladder diverticula following micturition presents special problems of interpretation, since a diverticulum may be regarded either as part of the bladder cavity, or as outside the functioning bladder.

4. The absence of residual urine is usually an observation of clinical value, but does not exclude intravesical obstruction or bladder dysfunction.

5. An isolated finding of residual urine requires confirmation before being considered significant.

**Complex Urodynamic Investigation**

The current techniques available for the investigation of urethral sphincteric dysfunction are difficult to interpret:

1. At rest the urethra is closed
2. The introduction of a catheter automatically introduces artefact
3. Measurements rely upon a patient being relaxed

Urethral pressure profilometry, although useful in the assessment of sympatholytic agents in drug trials, is not appropriate as a diagnostic technique. The dynamic evaluation of urethral sphincter function by the use of anal or skin-mounted electrodes is inaccurate. Accurate electromyographic evaluation of the urethral sphincter is possible with a concentric needle electrode, but is painful and cannot be carried out during voiding.

## URETHRAL PRESSURE MEASUREMENT

At rest the urethra is closed and this must be recognised when interpreting the results of urethral pressure studies. The urethral pressure and the urethral closure pressure are therefore idealised concepts which represent the ability of the urethra to prevent leakage. In current urodynamic practice, the urethral pressure is measured by a number of different techniques which do not always yield consistent values. Not only do the values differ with the method of measurement, but there is often lack of consistency for a single method—for example, the effect of catheter rotation when urethral pressure is measured by a catheter-mounted transducer, and the considerable artefacts which automatically result from the introduction of any catheter into the urethra.

### Technique

Measurements may be made at one point in the urethra over a period of time, or at several points along the urethra consecutively forming a *urethral pressure profile* (UPP).

At rest the *urethral pressure profile* denotes the intraluminal pressure

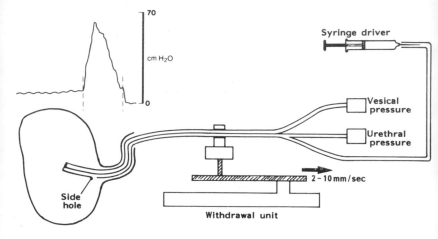

**Fig. 2.9** Schematic diagram of urethral pressure profilometry.

along the length of the urethra. All systems are zeroed at atmospheric pressure. For external transducers the reference point is the superior edge of the symphysis pubis. For catheter-mounted transducers the reference point is the transducer itself. Intravesical pressure should be measured to exclude a simultaneous detrusor contraction. The subtraction of intravesical pressure from urethral pressure produces the *urethral closure pressure profile* (Fig. 2.9).

Intraluminal urethral pressure may be measured:

1. At rest (the *storage phase*), with the bladder at any given volume—*resting urethral pressure profile* (UPP).

2. During coughing or straining—*stress urethral pressure profile*. The principle of this study is to measure the transmission of pressure from the abdominal cavity to the urethra. In stress incontinence this pressure transmission, which is thought to keep the normal urethra closed during stress, is inadequate. The urethral closure pressure becomes negative on coughing. A related but different test of bladder neck competence is the *fluid bridge test*, first described by Sutherst and Brown. This relies upon the continuity of fluid between

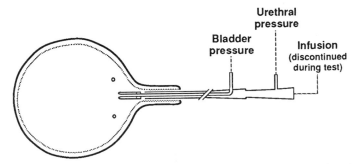

**Fig. 2.10**  The fluid bridge test. In this diagrammatic representation, the catheter is positioned with the lateral side hole just distal to the bladder neck. If the bladder neck is open, as demonstrated here, then there is a fluid column in continuity between the two sites and the urethral and bladder measurements become identical. (Abrams, Feneley and Torrens, 1983.)

the bladder and urethra, which results in the presence of bladder neck incompetence. Pressure transmission is measured down the infusion channel of a standard Brown/Wickham perfusion catheter, but with the perfusion switched off (Fig. 2.10).

3. During the process of voiding—*voiding urethral pressure profilometry* (VUPP). The VUPP is used to determine the pressure and site of urethral obstruction. Pressure is recorded in the urethra during voiding. The technique is similar to that used in the UPP measured during storage. Accurate interpretation of the VUPP depends on the simultaneous measurement of intravesical pressure and the measurement of pressure at a precisely localised point in the urethra. Localisation may be achieved by radio opaque marker on the catheter, which allows the pressure measurements to be related to a visualised point in the urethra.

### Practical points

The simultaneous recording of both intravesical and intraurethral pressures are essential during stress urethral profilometry.

The following information is essential when interpreting the results of such studies:

1. Infusion medium (liquid or gas)
2. Rate of infusion
3. Stationary, continuous or intermittent withdrawal
4. Rate of withdrawal
5. Bladder volume
6. Position of patient (supine, sitting or standing)

There are three principal techniques currently available:

1. The perfusion method as first described by Brown and Wickham (Fig 2.9) is most widely used. The catheter has a dual lumen, one lumen is used for pressure measurements and opens at the end of the catheter; the other for perfusion opens via two opposing side holes at a point 5 cm from the tip of the catheter. The catheter is constantly perfused at a set rate using a syringe pump (2–10 ml/min), whilst being withdrawn at a set speed (0.7 ml/s).

2. Catheter-mounted transducers eliminate errors associated with the use of fluid leaks and air bubbles, but introduce artefacts related to the orientation of the transducer.

3. Balloon catheter profilometry was first described by Enhorning and uses a small soft balloon mounted on a catheter. Pressure is transmitted by a fluid column to the external pressure transducer. This can measure urethral pressure accurately, but is more difficult to use than the other two methods.

Whatever method is used, it is essential to use sufficiently sensitive recording apparatus.

**Definitions** (Fig 2.11 referring to profiles measured in storage phase)

*Maximum urethral pressure* is the maximum pressure of the measured profile.

*Maximum urethral closure pressure* is the maximum difference between the urethral pressure and the intravesical pressure.

*Functional profile length* is the length of the urethra along which the urethral pressure exceeds intravesical pressure.

*Functional profile length (on stress)* is the length over which the urethral pressure exceeds the intravesical pressure on stress.

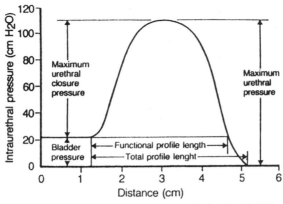

**Fig. 2.11** Diagram of a female urethral pressure profile (static) with ICS recommended nomenclature. (Reproduced with permission from the Scandinavian Journal of Urology and Nephrology, 114, 1988.)

***Pressure 'transmission' ratio*** is the increment in urethral pressure on stress as a percentage of the simultaneously recorded increment in intravesical pressure. For stress profiles obtained during coughing, pressure transmission ratios can be obtained at any point along the urethra. If single values are given, the position in the urethra should be stated. If several pressure transmission ratios are defined at different points along the urethra, a pressure 'transmission' profile is obtained. During 'cough profiles' the amplitude of the cough should be stated if possible.

## Comment

Urethral pressure profilometry has, in recent years, enjoyed a disproportionate amount of attention. The results obtained are extremely susceptible to experimental artefacts and the degree of relaxation of the patient. In particular, it must be remembered that this study can be distressingly uncomfortable for the patients—especially males.

The information gained from urethral pressure measurements in the storage phase is of limited value in the assessment of voiding

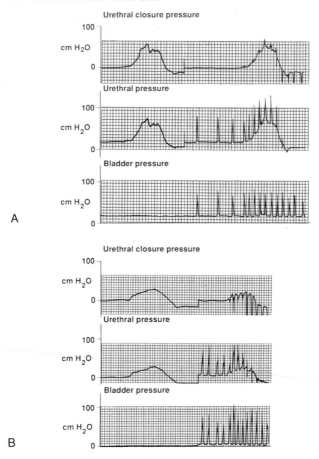

**Fig. 2.12** A. This demonstrates a urethral pressure profile at rest (to the left) and during coughing (to the right) in a normal female. During coughing there is the transmission of intra-abdominal pressure (represented by bladder trace) to the urethra, in all except the distal portion of the profile, with good preservation of the shape of the urethral tract. B. A pair of urethral pressure traces in a patient with genuine stress incontinence. The pressure trace is flattened as contrasted to normal and during coughing there is lack of normal transmission of the intra-abdominal pressure, resulting in a negative deflection of the urethral pressure trace. This abnormal response is the consequence of a prolapse of the urethra within a cystourethrocele. (Abrams, Feneley, Torrens, 1983.)

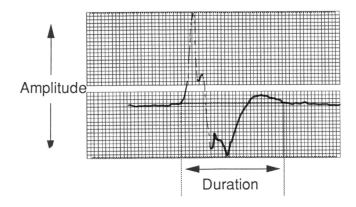

Amplitude

Duration

**Fig. 2.13**   Muscle action potential from urethral sphincter electromyogram.

disorders. Total profile length is not generally regarded as a useful parameter.

VUPP is not yet fully developed as a technique and a number of technical, as well as clinical, problems need to be solved before the VUPP is widely used.

## NEUROPHYSIOLOGICAL INVESTIGATION

### A. Electromyography

Electromyography (EMG) is the study of electrical potentials generated by the depolarisation of muscle and, in this context, refers to urethral sphincter striated muscle EMG. The functional unit in EMG is the motor unit. This is comprised of a single motor neurone and the muscle fibres which results from activation of a single anterior horn cell (Fig 2.13). Muscle action potentials may be detected either by needle electrodes, or by surface electrodes.

*Technique*

Needle electrodes (concentric, bipolar, monopolar, single fibre) are placed directly into the muscle mass and permit visualisation of the individual motor unit action potentials (Fig 2.13).

Surface electrodes (skin, anal plug, catheter) are applied to an epithelial surface as close to the muscle under study as possible. Surface electrodes detect the action potentials from groups of adjacent motor units underlying the recording surface; they can be difficult to secure adequately and provide less reproducible results.

### Practical points

EMG potentials may be displayed on an oscilloscope screen or played through audio amplifiers. A permanent record of EMG potentials can only be made using a chart recorder with a high frequency response (in the range of 10 kHz).

The interpretation of needle EMG results requires the services of a skilled investigator.

### Comment

EMG should be interpreted in the light of the patient's symptoms, physical findings and urological and urodynamic investigations. The main clinical indication for EMG studies is as an adjunct to videocystometrography to distinguish between striated and smooth muscle in distal urethral obstruction of a neuropathic type. Other EMG studies provide interesting scientific information, which however, rarely alters the clinical management of patients.

## B. Nerve conduction studies

Nerve conduction studies involve stimulation of a peripheral nerve and recording the time for a response to occur in muscle, innervated by the nerve under study.

## C. Reflex latencies

Reflect latencies require stimulation of sensory fields and recordings from the muscle which contracts reflexly in response to the stimulation. Such responses are a test of reflex arcs, which comprise both afferent and efferent limbs and a synaptic region within the central nervous system. The reflex latency expresses the nerve conduction velocity in both limbs of the arc and the integrity of the central nervous system at the level of the synapse(s). Increased reflex latency may occur as a result of slowed afferent or efferent nerve conduction, or due to central nervous system conduction delays.

## D. Sensory testing

Limited information, of a subjective nature, may be obtained during cystometry by recording such parameters as the first desire to micturate, urgency or pain. However, sensory function in the lower urinary tract can be assessed by semi-objective tests, which rely upon the measurement of urethral and/or vesical sensory thresholds to a standard applied stimulus such as a known electrical current.

The *vesical/urethral sensory threshold* is defined as the least current which consistently produces a sensation perceived by the subject during stimulation at the site under investigation; the absolute values will vary in relation to the site of the stimulus, the characteristics of the equipment and the stimulation parameters.

## UPPER URINARY TRACT URODYNAMICS—
## THE WHITAKER TEST

Upper tract obstruction often goes unrecognised. The clinical indications for functional studies are chronic loin pain and/or deteriorating renal function where an obstructing ureteric lesion has not been excluded, or where the significance of an obstructing lesion is in doubt. Diuresis excretory urography has little to offer as the anatomical demonstration of a dilated system neither confirms nor excludes obstruction. Diuresis renography, radionuclide parenchymal transit times and pressure flow studies are the techniques now used to investigate equivocally obstructed kidneys. Nuclear medicine studies are of particular importance in providing an assessment of differential renal function and are essential in serial follow up.

The upper urinary tract is a highly distensible system protected, in normal circumstances, from the intermittent high pressure generated by the bladder by the competent vesicoureteric junction. Under normal circumstances, urine accumulates in the renal pelvis at a resting pressure of less than 5 cm $H_2O$. The pelvic pressure rises to 10 cm $H_2O$ once distended, and urine enters the ureter to be transported as a bolus to the bladder by ureteric peristalsis at pressures between 20–60 cm $H_2O$. Efficient peristalsis is dependent upon the ureteric walls being able to oppose. Ureteric dilation, whether obstructive or not, or disorders of wall mobility prevent the ureteric walls opposing, compromising the efficient transport of urine and tubular flow. The normal response of the upper tract to obstruction at, or above, the vesicoureteric junction is an increase in the rate of ureteric and pelvic peristalsis and eventual dilatation. Dilatation causes discoordinated peristalsis and inefficient transport of urine. As flow is reduced down the ureter, pressure rises are first transmitted to the collecting ducts, then along the tubules to the glomeruli. If there is not parallel increase in the glomerular hydrostatic pressure, filtration will eventually stop.

Pressure flow studies involve the perfusion of the kidney with contrast at a known rate, whilst simultaneously measuring the pressure within the renal pelvis and bladder. Significant rises in pressure are indicative of obstruction, whilst free drainage at low pressure excludes obstruction.

## Technique

The Whitaker test is performed in the conscious patient at least 24 hours after insertion of a nephrostomy tube. Bladder pressure is measured via a urethral catheter connected to a transducer. Renal pelvic pressure can be measured through a nephrostomy tube, or through a needle placed in the collecting system at antegrade pyelography. Puncture technique needs to be as good as any leak for the collecting system degrades the information that pressure studies will provide. Through one arm of a 'Y' connector, dilute contrast

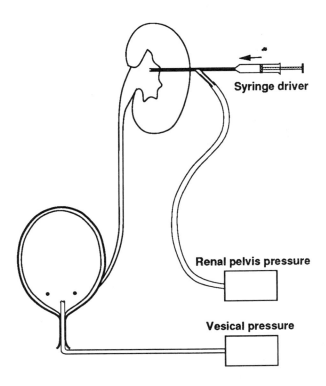

**Fig. 2.14** Schematic representation of the Whitaker test.

is infused at an initial rate of 10 ml/min, whilst the other arm of the 'Y' is connected to a pressure transducer recording renal pelvic pressure in response to perfusion. Perfusion at 10 ml/min is considerably in excess of physiological rates. The bladder pressure is continuously recorded and the subtracted pressure (pelvic pressure−bladder pressure) automatically calculated. Such manometric equipment is available in any department performing lower urinary tract urodynamics. Simultaneous fluoroscopy defines the anatomy of the upper tract and spot films can be taken (Fig. 2.14).

**Practical points**

1. Using this technique, a pressure difference between the upper and lower urinary tract of less than 15 cm $H_2O$ excludes obstruction. If the renal pelvic pressure exceeds the bladder pressure by more than 22 cm $H_2O$, obstruction is confirmed.

2. Pressure differentials between 15 and 22 cm $H_2O$ lie in the equivocal range. If both the bladder and pelvic pressure rise equally together, vesicoureteric reflux has occurred.

3. Higher rates of perfusion have been advocated, but are of debateable clinical usefulness.

4. In the patient with a urinary diversion, e.g. ileal loop, loin pain is quite frequent because of the high pressures generated by bowel peristalsis refluxing up the reinplanted ureters. The extent of this can easily be assessed by upper tract urodynamics.

**Comment**

The principal value of upper tract urodynamics lies in allowing an accurate objective assessment as to whether there is obstruction to renal drainage. It is an invasive procedure, since a percutaneous nephrostomy tract is required and therefore its use should be reserved for the case where other investigations, such as excretory urography or isotope renography, have produced equivocal results.

## DISORDERS OF THE LOWER URINARY TRACT

Disorders of the lower urinary tract can best be subdivided into *disorders of sensation* and *disorders of motor function*, each of these may affect the *detrusor muscle* or the *urethra* (bladder neck mechanism, distal urethral sphincter mechanism, prostate), each of which may be:—*normal, overactive, underactive*

**Disorders of sensation**

These represent an important, yet poorly understood, group of conditions where investigation is restricted by our limited knowledge as to the structural and physiological basis for the perception of sensation in the lower urinary tract and further hampered by the totally subjective nature of sensation. Previous workers have attempted to quantify sensation by the use of objective or semi-objective tests for sensory function, such as evoked potentials or electrical threshold studies. At present, disorders of sensation are usually assessed by questioning the patient as to voiding pattern, and the symptoms of discomfort are assessed during clinical questioning or during cystometry. Since the majority of sensory disorders remain of idiopathic aetiology, this diagnosis is best considered as being one of exclusion—other vesical or urethral pathologies (tumour, stone, infective, abnormalities of detrusor function) must first be excluded. In general terms, sensation can be subdivided as follows: *normal, hypersensitive, hyposensitive, absent.*

### Definitions

The majority of these relate to cystometry (intravesical pressure measurements).

**First sensation of filling.** Very subjective, a rather variable and unreliable symptom.

**First desire to void.** Can be difficult to interpret, very subjective.

**Strong desire to void.** Indicates maximum bladder capacity and signals the end of bladder filling during cystometry.

**Pain.** Pain during bladder filling or micturition is abnormal. Note should be taken of its site and character.

## Disorders of detrusor motor function

Assessment of detrusor function requires the use of cystometry and it must be remembered, not only that it may be different during filling and voiding, but that the classification may change between these two phases. It must be remembered that detrusor function should be considered in the context of coexisting urethral function, but is often the primary cause of significant functional disruption.

Detrusor function may be: *normal* (stable), *overactive*, *underactive* (hypocontractile), *acontractile*.

## Definitions

**Stable detrusor function.** During filling the bladder contents increase in volume without a significant corresponding rise in pressure.

**Normal detrusor contractility.** Normal voiding occurs by a sustained detrusor contraction, which can be initiated and suppressed voluntarily and results in complete bladder emptying over a normal timespan; the magnitude of the recorded detrusor pressure rise is dependent on the outlet resistance.

**Overactive detrusor function.** Involuntary detrusor contractions during bladder filling, either spontaneous or provoked by rapid filling (provocation cystometry), alterations in posture, exercise or coughing.

'**The unstable detrusor** is one that is shown objectively to contract either spontaneously or on provocation during the filling phase while the patient is attempting to inhibit micturition. The unstable detrusor may be asymptomatic and its presence does not necessarily imply a neurological disorder' (ICS).

**Detrusor hyperreflexia.** Detrusor hyperactivity in the presence of a documented neurological disorder.

**Low-compliance.** During normal bladder filling little or no significant rise in pressure occurs so-called normal compliance. Although the term low-compliance is applied to a gradual rise in detrusor pressure during bladder filling and is usually taken to imply a poorly distensible bladder, e.g. a shrunken fibrotic bladder complicating interstitial cystitis or after radiotherapy, it must be remembered that both detrusor instability and hyperreflexia are forms of low compliance and that, at present, there is insufficient data to define normal, high and low compliance.

**Underactive (hypocontractile) detrusor function.** This is taken to be referring to detrusor activity during micturition. The term underactive applies to all situations where a detrusor contraction is inadequate to produce emptying of the bladder.

***Acontractile detrusor.*** No contractile activity is evident on urodynamic investigation.

***Areflexic detrusor.*** Acontractility resulting from an abnormality of the central nervous system. A specific type occurs with lesions of the conus medullaris or sacral nerve outflow and is known as a *decentralised detrusor*, where the peripheral ganglia in the wall of the bladder are preserved and peripheral nerves are therefore intact. This subgroup is characterised by involuntary intravesical pressure fluctuations of low amplitude, sometimes called 'autonomous waves'.

## Disorders of bladder outflow tract function

The urethral closure mechanism, including intrinsic urethral muscle, and the sphincteric mechanisms (bladder neck and distal urethral) may best be considered separately depending upon the phase of bladder function (either storage or voiding).

Urethral function during storage: *normal, incompetent, underactive, absent.*

### Definitions

***Normal urethral closure mechanism.*** This maintains a positive urethral closure pressure, which is sufficient even in the presence of increased intra-abdominal pressure to maintain continence.

***Incompetent urethral closure mechanism.*** This allows leakage, even in the absence of detrusor contraction. It may result from damage to either the urethra itself and/or the associated sphincteric mechanisms.

Urethral function during micturition: *normal, obstructive, over-activity, mechanical.*

*The normal urethra* opens to allow the bladder to be emptied.

***Obstruction due to urethral overactivity.*** The urethral closure mechanism contracts against a detrusor contraction or fails to open on attempted micturition, when this occurs in the absence of documented neurological disease it is known as *dysfunctional voiding.*

***Detrusor/urethral dyssynergia.*** Synchronous contraction of detrusor and urethra, which can be further subdivided depending on the structures involved.

***Destrusor/bladder neck dyssynergia.*** This refers to a detrusor contraction concurrent with a failure for there to be complete bladder neck opening on micturition. Although rare in the population, it is a common cause of voiding dysfunction in the younger male. In this context it is important to realise that, in recent years, it has been increasingly recognised that an important component of prostatic obstruction results from the contraction of smooth muscle within the pathologically enlarged prostate.

***Detrusor/sphincter dyssynergia (DSD).*** This describes a detrusor contraction concurrent with an involuntary contraction of the urethral and/or periurethral striated smooth muscle. No similar term has been elaborated for corresponding detrusor/distal urethral smooth muscle dyssynergia. Obstructive overactivity of the striated urethral sphincter muscle may occur in the absence of detrusor contraction, but is not DSD. DSD is usually associated with neurological disorders and, in the absence of a documented neurological deficit, this diagnosis would need to be treated with caution.

***Obstruction due to mechanical obstruction.*** This is uncommon in women and is by far the commonest cause in the male population. The likeliest causes are urethral stricture or prostatic enlargement.

Mechanical obstruction can arise both as a direct consequence of anatomical factors, e.g. prostatic enlargement due to adenomatous hyperplasia, and under the influence of the neural control mechanisms, e.g. relief of obstruction by the use of $\alpha$-adrenoceptor blockade on the prostate.

## STANDARDISATION

Tables 2.1 and 2.2 give the units of measurement and standardised symbols used in urodynamics.

**Table 2.1** Units of measurement and standardised symbols used in urodynamics

| Quantity | Acceptable unit | Symbol |
|----------|-----------------|--------|
| Volume | millilitre | ml |
| Time | second | s |
| Flow rate | millilitres/second | $ml.s^{-1}$ |
| Pressure | centimetres of water* | $cmH_2O$ |
| Length | metres or submultiples | m, cm, mm |
| Velocity | metres/second or submultiples | $m.s^{-1}$, $cm.s^{-1}$ |
| Temperature | degrees Celsius | $°C$ |

* The SI unit is the pascal (Pa), but it is only practical at present to calibrate our instruments in cm $H_2O$. One centimetre of water pressure is approximately equal to 100 pascals (1 cm $H_2O$=98.07 Pa=0.098 kPa).

**Table 2.2** List of symbols

| Basic symbols | | Urological qualifiers | | Value | |
|---------------|---|----------------------|-----|-------|-----|
| Pressure | $p$ | Bladder | ves | Maximum | max |
| Volume | $V$ | Urethra | ura | Minimum | min |
| Flow rate | $Q$ | Ureter | ure | Average | ave |
| Velocity | $v$ | Detrusor | det | Isovolumetric | isv |
| Time | $t$ | Abdomen | abd | Isotonic | ist |
| Temperature | $T$ | External stream | ext | Isobaric | isb |
| Length | $l$ | | | Isometric | ism |
| Area | $A$ | | | | |
| Diameter | $d$ | | | | |
| Force | $F$ | | | | |
| Energy | $E$ | | | | |
| Power | $P$ | | | | |
| Compliance | $C$ | | | | |
| Work | $W$ | | | | |
| Energy per unit volume | $e$ | | | | |

Examples: $p_{det.max}$=maximum detrusor pressure

$e_{.ext}$=kinetic energy per unit volume in the external stream

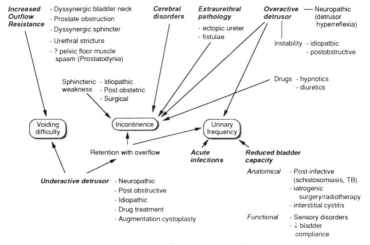

**Fig. 2.15** Schematic representation of the large number of potential aetiologies which can produce urinary symptoms.

## THE CLINICAL PROBLEM

The major problems of micturition encountered in urological practice can be considered in three main groups:

1. Difficulty voiding
2. Urinary incontinence
3. Voiding frequency.

A number of aetiological factors can result in one of these three symptoms and are summarised in Figure 2.15. From the preceding discussion, it is evident that urodynamic evaluation is essential for the accurate investigation of patients. Since it is not possible here to attempt more than a brief summary of this subject, comprehensive reviews should be consulted for more detailed information.

# 3. Specialised urodynamics

## THE NEUROPATHIC BLADDER

Vesicourethral dysfunction is a common feature of many systemic and local neurological conditions. The interpretation of urodynamics in such complex cases is often difficult and is best performed in specialist centres using VCMG. Neurological conditions may alter vesicourethral function by impairment of the following mechanisms:

1. Detrusor activity
2. Striated sphincter activity
3. Bladder and/or urethral sensation
4. Urethral smooth muscle activity

Alterations of the above may occur in isolation or in combination in neurological conditions. It should also be appreciated that identical abnormalities may also occur without clinical evidence of neurological deficit.

*1. Detrusor activity.* Detrusor activity may be absent or diminished in cases where there are lesions of the cell bodies, or parasympathetic efferents to the bladder from the sacral roots (S 2,3,4). This may be due to trauma to the spinal cord or pelvic nerves, or destruction of the cord segment by lesions such as those associated with multiple sclerosis.

Detrusor overactivity (hyperreflexia) may result when there is damage above the level of the sacral cord leading to loss of voluntary control of the detrusor. This may be due to spina bifida, cerebrovascular accident, trauma, multiple sclerosis, tumour or other neurological disease. Detrusor contractions may be spontaneous or provoked by bladder filling (as in the *automatic bladder*).

**2. *Striated sphincter activity*.** The striated muscle element of the distal urethral sphincter mechanism may fail to relax during voiding and this is called detrusor-sphincter dyssynergia. This results from suprasacral lesions. Weakness of the striated sphincter muscle may occur with lesions distal to, or including its sacral nerve supply. The smooth muscle element of the urethral sphincter mechanism may also be disturbed with neurological lesions.

**3. *Bladder and/or urethral sensation*.** Loss of sensation within the bladder or urethra may occur after local damage to pelvic nerves or the spinal cord.

Since so many different aspects of vesicourethral function may be impaired in neurological conditions, interpretation may be difficult. The most important points to clarify in clinical practice are the presence or absence of detrusor hyperreflexia and the behaviour of the distal urethral sphincter mechanism during voiding. High-pressure bladders with detrusor-sphincter dyssynergia are prone to develop vesicoureteric reflux, which may ultimately lead to renal impairment. This can be clearly demonstrated by VCMG. Preservation of renal function is of utmost importance in the management of patients with chronic neurological conditions. Detrusor hyperreflexia in isolation may be treated in the same way as detrusor instability (see Chapter 4).

**4. *Urethral smooth muscle activity*.** Detrusor-sphincter dyssynergia may require surgical treatment to the sphincter in the form of sphincterotomy or stent insertion and the incontinence that should result from these procedures can be controlled by implantation of an artificial urinary sphincter (e.g. Brantley Scott prosthesis).

## CYSTOPLASTY URODYNAMICS

Enterocystoplasty using small or large bowel has become increasingly popular as a treatment for bladder dysfunction. All cases in whom such a procedure is planned should undergo careful urodynamic evaluation prior to the operation. 'Clam' cystoplasty, using a segment of terminal ileum, is now popular as a treatment for detrusor hyperreflexia and primary detrusor instability. Augmentation cystoplasty using caecum, colon, or a pouch constructed from segments of ileum, is a useful technique for increasing the bladder capacity in cases where the capacity is restricted due to interstitial cystitis, postirradiation fibrosis or tuberculous contracture. Also, some cases of bladder carcinoma are suitable for subtotal cystectomy and augmentation cystoplasty using similar techniques. Augmentation cystoplasty can be performed using intact segments of bowel, detubularised bowel (in which the tubular structure is surgically altered), or pouches.

Following cystoplasty some cases will experience persistent or new symptoms, such as urinary frequency and/or incontinence, voiding difficulty, or recurrent urinary tract infections. VCMG is important in the evaluation of such cases. The bowel segments usually peristalse as they would in their usual situation. Voiding is achieved by abdominal straining, which is more efficient when coincident with peristaltic contractions. High-pressure peristaltic contractions may lead to urinary frequency, urgency and incontinence. This is more likely to occur when nondetubularised bowel segments are used, but is, however, a rare occurrence.

VCMG is particularly useful in the assessment of complicated postcystoplasty cases and attention can be paid to several important factors. Is the cystoplasty overactive? Is this overactivity associated with outflow obstruction? Is incontinence due to hyperactivity of the bowel segment or impaired outflow resistance? The presence or absence of a postmicturition residual is better assessed by USCD, but VCMG may clarify the aetiology.

Overactive cystoplasties associated with outflow obstruction are best treated by relief of obstruction in the first instance. In the female this usually means urethral dilatation, while in the male bladder neck incision or transurethral prostatectomy may be indicated. Mucus production by the bowel segment can lead to the formation of mucus plugs that may cause intermittent obstruction. It has recently been shown that a regular intake of cranberry juice can lead to a decrease in mucus production and hence prevent such obstruction. Hyperactive cystoplasties without obstruction initially are best treated by pharmacotherapy. In the authors' experience Terodiline and Oxybutynin are not generally helpful in treating hyperactive cystoplasties. Also, drugs such as Mebeverine (Colofac) that are administered orally as a treatment for irritable colon are not sufficiently well absorbed to act upon bowel segments separated from the alimentary tract and are therefore not efficacious in the treatment of hyperactive cystoplasties. If drug therapy fails and the symptoms resulting from overactivity of the cystoplasty are sufficiently severe then further surgery is indicated. It is often most convenient to add a patch of small bowel to the side of the cystoplasty, using the same concept as the 'clam' cystoplasty.

Underactivity or absent peristalsis of cystoplasties is more likely to occur after detubularisation of the bowel segment. Many cases, particularly females, are able to void to completion by abdominal straining and hence suffer no adverse symptoms. However, under-active cystoplasties may be associated with large postmicturition residual urine, which in turn may lead to recurrent urinary tract infections. This problem is more likely to occur in males in whom the outflow resistance is greater and hence abdominal straining is less efficient. When large residuals are associated with recurrent infections, intermittent self-catheterisation is often indicated and may relieve symptoms.

# 4. Voiding difficulties—prostatic obstruction and urethral strictures

## INTRODUCTION

Voiding difficulty is the commonest cause of symptoms prompting men to present to urologists. This is not surprising in view of the common prevalence of prostatic outflow obstruction in the male population. Voiding difficulty is an uncommon cause for referral of women to a urologist. The majority of these female patients will have a neuropathic disorder affecting the bladder.

Although the majority of causes of voiding difficulty in men are due to *increased outflow resistance* resulting from obstruction at the level of the bladder neck, the prostate, or a urethral stricture, it must be remembered that voiding difficulty may also result from *detrusor muscle failure*, which may either be primary or secondary to the outflow obstruction (Fig. 4.1).

## INCREASED OUTFLOW RESISTANCE

### Urethral strictures

These occur usually in male patients who present with a history of diminished stream (once the urethral calibre is reduced below 11 Ch) with a prolonged slow flow rate. Once suspected, they are best demonstrated by urethrography. Therapy consists of urethral dilatation, urethrotomy, urethroplasty, or urethral stent insertion.

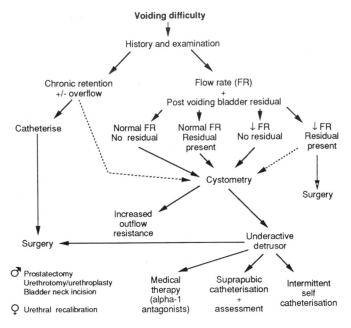

**Fig. 4.1** Flow diagram showing management of voiding disorders.

## Prostatic obstruction

Both benign and malignant enlargement of the prostate are increasingly common with advancing age in the elderly male. Benign prostatic hyperplasia is increasingly common as a histological diagnosis over the age of puberty and becomes an important cause of obstructive symptoms from the sixth decade of life onwards. Prostatic adenocarcinoma is the sixth commonest neoplasm in the UK and the most important tumour of the male genitourinary tract. Not surprisingly, benign and malignant disease often coexist, but the relationship appears to be coincidental. Although both conditions are under the trophic influence of the male hormone testosterone, carcinoma usually originates in the peripheral zone of the gland and benign adenomata in the periurethral central zone.

Detrusor instability occurs in up to 70% of men presenting with prostatic outflow obstruction. Although detrusor instability is more common with increasing age, a causal link between the instability and outlet obstruction is suggested by the observation that in up to two-thirds of patients the detrusor instability will resolve following surgical relief of the obstruction.

Acute retention is a common clinical problem and indeed usually contributes significantly to the clinical workload of a urologist in a district general hospital. Usually, acute retention supervenes in a case with a pre-existing history of prostatic outflow obstruction, although this may not always be the case. The current doctrine is that it may be exacerbated by increased sympathetic stimulation acting upon the bladder and outflow tract, in particular, the prostatic urethra. Common precipitating factors implicated are stress, alcohol consumption, or a cold environmental temperature.

*History and examination*

The classical symptoms of so-called *prostatism* can be subdivided into two main groups:

***Irritative*** — resulting from detrusor instability — frequency, nocturia, urgency, urge incontinence.

***Obstructive:*** hesitancy, poor stream, feeling of incomplete bladder emptying, terminal dribble.

The symptom of postmicturition dribble is not due to obstruction, but results from bulbar pooling and therefore is common in the elderly male, following urethroplasty, and in bladder neck obstruction.

Clinical examination may reveal a palpable bladder and thereby confirm the diagnosis of urinary retention. Digital rectal examination is essential, since a malignant neoplasm may be diagnosed, and transrectal ultrasound with biopsy can be useful in confirming this.

*Urodynamics*

In the majority of cases a flow rate and urinary residual estimation are sufficient to confirm the diagnosis of prostatic obstruction. Normal voiding can be maintained during the early stages of the development of prostatic obstruction, by a compensatory increase in voiding detrusor pressure. It must, however, be remembered that a flow rate by itself will not be able to differentiate between high pressure/low flow and low pressure/low flow. This distinction is important, since many patients who have an unsatisfactory result with previous prostatic surgery will fall into the latter category. More detailed urodynamic investigation is therefore essential in the patient where a flow rate is equivocal or previous surgery has failed, or left residual symptoms such as incontinence (to differentiate between detrusor instability and sphincteric weakness). The typical CMG/VCMG appearances are demonstrated here (Fig. 4.2).

*Treatment*

The treatment of prostatic obstruction is traditionally surgical resection of obstructive prostatic tissue. Although conventional surgery still remains the treatment of choice, a number of surgical alternatives have been explored in recent years. These include cold punch prostatectomy, cryosurgery, microwave therapy, balloon dilatation, ultrasonic cavitation, mechanical pulverisation, intra-urethral prostatic stent insertion.

In recent years there has been increasing recognition that pharmacotherapy may be beneficial; this can be subdivided into drugs which shrink prostate and those which relax it. The former group of agents act by inhibiting the action of testosterone on the prostate—a chemical castration (oestrogens and LHRH analogues); an unacceptable consequence of their use is that they result in feminisation and symptoms such as loss of libido resulting from a loss of androgen drive.

More promising therapy is provided by the $5\alpha$-reductase inhibitors, which specifically inhibit the conversion of testosterone into its active

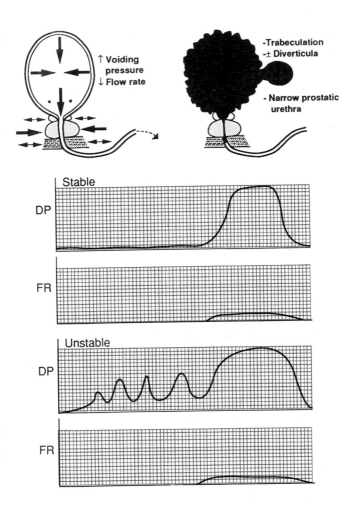

**Fig. 4.2** Prostate outflow obstruction.

form dihydrotestosterone within the prostate, thereby avoiding unwanted systemic side-effects. The second category of drugs relax prostatic musculature by inhibition of the contractile action of sympathetic nerves, which act via stimulation of $\alpha_1$-adrenoceptors. These $\alpha_1$-antagonists have a useful therapeutic role in patients who are unfit for surgery, unwilling to undergo surgery and where surgery awaits at the end of a long waiting list.

Many of these new therapies are currently under evaluation, but to date none have proven to be a viable alternative to TURP in routine clinical practice.

## Obstruction due to urethral overactivity

During normal voiding, the urethra relaxes synchronously with contraction of the detrusor muscle. Should, for any reason, there be failure of relaxation of the urethra and in particular its associated sphincter mechanisms then the condition of the dysfunctional voiding occurs. Three main types of such dysfunctional voiding are recognised.

1.  Failure of the bladder neck mechanism to relax—detrusor/ bladder neck dyssynergia, otherwise known as bladder neck obstruction.

2.  Detrusor sphincter dyssynergia, which complicates a number of neurological disorders affecting the lower urinary tract—commonly Parkinson's disease and multiple sclerosis.

3.  Detrusor/urethral dyssynergia—a little recognised condition primarily affecting young women, where the urethral sphincter mechanism fails to relax.

## History and examination

The brief descriptions given above should be borne in mind when taking a history in any patient with outflow obstruction. Associated neurological symptoms and signs should alert one to the possibility of detrusor sphincter dyssynergia—best demonstrated on video-cystometry (Fig. 4.3); with the synchronous use of electromyo-

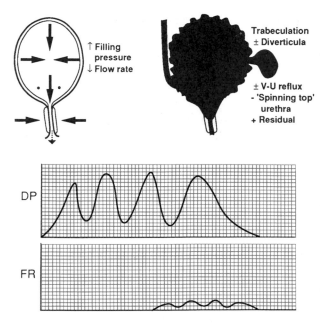

**Fig. 4.3** Detrusor/sphincter dyssynergia.

graphy. The patient with bladder neck dyssynergia usually presents, either with voiding difficulty in the third or fourth decade of life or a complication of outflow obstruction such as the urinary tract infection. Further questioning will often reveal a lifelong history of diminished urinary stream. Videocystometry will demonstrate findings suggestive of bladder outflow obstruction and, in particular, will show the trapping of contrast at the bladder neck on carrying out a stop test (Fig. 4.4). We have recently found that these patients invariably have a characteristic lucent area seen on transrectal ultrasound scans of the bladder neck. Detrusor/urethral dyssynergia effects young women who present with a history of difficulty voiding which is lifelong and often with associated secondary detrusor failure. Many of these women have an associated hormonal problem (Stein-

Leventhal syndrome—hirsutism/polycystic ovaries/amenorrhoea) and it has recently been recognised that there are characteristic motor unit appearances on electromyography.

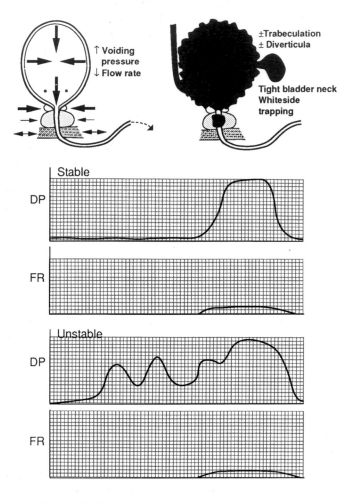

**Fig. 4.4** Detrusor/bladder neck dyssynergia.

## Treatment

The treatment of detrusor sphincter dyssynergia is primarily supportive and intermittent self-catheterisation, if feasible (good hand motor function), has a particular value. In some patients with a neurological cause for such symptoms, a sphincterotomy is necessary, which renders the patient incontinent—they are then managed with an incontinence appliance; recently a permanently implanted urethral stent has been found to be a satisfactory alternative.

### Problems

1. The difficulty arises in the elderly male patient with Parkinson's disease where detrusor sphincter dyssynergia may coexist with prostate obstruction. A useful therapeutic manoeuvre in these cases is to insert an intraurethral prostatic stent which will treat the prostate obstruction and will thereby enable a distinction between these two conditions to be made.

2. Detrusor-bladder neck dyssynergia is easily treated by endoscopic incision of the bladder, but there is a risk of damaging the function of the sphincter mechanism with secondary retrograde ejaculation and, in the young male where this poses a problem by impairing fertility, a therapeutic trial of $\alpha_1$-blockade is worthwhile.

3. Although detrusor/urethral dyssynergia can now be clearly defined on the basis of electromyographic appearances, the treatment of this remains unsatisfactory and is similar to that for detrusor/sphincter dyssynergia, relying upon measures such as urethral dilatation and intermittent self-catheterisation; hormonal manipulation has proven to be unsuccessful in these patients.

## DETRUSOR FAILURE
## (UNDERACTIVE DETRUSOR FUNCTION)

The possibility of hypocontractile detrusor function should be considered in any patient who presents with voiding difficulty. Although the objective demonstration of this condition relies upon the use of formal cystometry, the condition must always be suspected in any patient presenting with incontinence, particularly the elderly male since the diagnosis here may be chronic retention with overflow incontinence.

## CHRONIC RETENTION

This refers to a chronically distended bladder, whether resulting from a known pathology such as prostate obstruction, urethral stricture, or a lower motor neurone lesion affecting the bladder. In a number of cases chronic retention is idiopathic and, indeed, many of the patients presenting with chronic retention in the presence of presumed prostatic obstruction have small prostate glands and may have an underlying predisposition to develop chronic retention—as yet unidentified. There is a small, but distinct, group of middle-aged elderly female patients who present with acute retention of urine, usually after surgery, and who often vigorously deny any previous history of voiding difficulty. In some of these patients, however, it is possible to elicit a previous history of infrequent voiding (camel bladder). Urodynamic investigation demonstrates an underactive detrusor with chronic retention.

### Urodynamics

Urodynamic appearances of detrusor hypocontractility are demonstrated here (Fig. 4.5).

### Treatment

The correction of the underactive detrusor is aimed at correction of any underlying aetiology; in the absence of a neurological deficit in the male a relative obstruction at the prostate level is presumed to be present.

*Therapeutic measures* are therefore directed at ensuring that the bladder is emptied regularly to prevent back pressure and subsequent damage to the upper tracts. In the male patient prostatic resection is usually carried out and in the female patient a urethral recalibra-

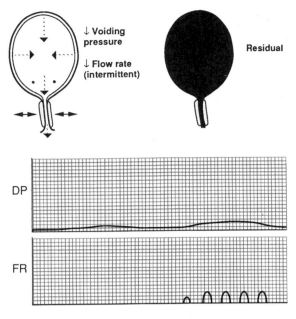

**Fig. 4.5.** Underactive detrusor.

tion. The placement of a suprapubic catheter, particularly in patients with neurological deficit which is potentially reversible, is important since this decompresses the detrusor, preventing any further damage by distention to the detrusor muscle fibres and enabling careful assessment of post-operative postvoiding intravesical residuals to be made. Long-term therapeutic measures include the use of intermittent self-catheterisation and the use of pharmacotherapy aimed at relaxing the outflow tract (e.g. $\alpha_1$ antagonists). Bladder training can be useful particularly in the infrequent voiders, where they are instructed to void by the clock (for instance, 2-hourly). The follow-up of patients is facilitated by the careful monitoring of intravesical residuals by the use of ultrasound (the ultrasound cystodynamogram).

# 5. Incontinence

## INTRODUCTION

Urinary incontinence is an involuntary loss of urine that may leak per urethram or through an extraurethral route. The latter situation may be congenital, such as found with ectopic ureter, or may be iatrogenic as in vesico-vaginal fistula. Urinary incontinence may be a symptom or a sign when demonstrated during examination or urodynamics.

Urinary incontinence is a distressing affliction that predominantly affects elderly females. Incontinence carries a considerable social stigma that only recently has improved due to an increased awareness of the problem, although many sufferers are still reluctant to seek advice or treatment. Some patients are able to overcome incontinence by passing urine frequently, or by restricting their fluid intake and physical activities that may cause the problem. Others cope with incontinence by wearing pads or other devices. All patients with incontinence should be encouraged to seek expert medical advice, since the majority of cases are amenable to some form of therapy that should improve their symptoms. A careful medical history should be taken with particular emphasis on the factors that induce leakage, previous obstetric history, surgical history and drug therapy. Clinical examination may reveal palpable enlargement of the bladder, or stress leakage with or without prolapse when the patient coughs. Urodynamic evaluation is particularly important in the assessment of all forms of incontinence, although it is not always necessary in

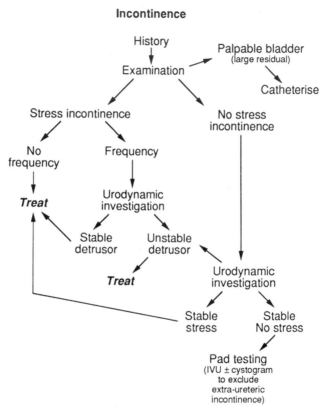

**Fig. 5.1** Flow diagram showing the management of urinary incontinence.

straightforward cases of stress incontinence. The basic steps that should be taken in the investigation of incontinence are shown in Figure 5.1. It is most important initially to differentiate incontinence due to detrusor overactivity from incontinence due to inadequate outflow resistance and it should also be appreciated that these phenomena may coexist.

## GENUINE STRESS INCONTINENCE

Genuine stress incontinence (GSI) is defined as incontinence associated with activities such as coughing, sneezing, running, jumping and sexual intercourse that increase intra-abdominal pressure and hence, also, the intra-vesical pressure leading to urine leak. The amount of urine that leaks out is usually quite small. This is predominantly a female problem because of the short female urethra and single sphincter mechanism. It is particularly common in elderly multiparous women who have had traumatic or prolonged vaginal deliveries. GSI is due to reduced outflow resistance, which may be at the level of the bladder neck, striated urethral sphincter, or both of these. It is now evident that continence in the female is dependent on the coexistence of a functioning urethral sphincter mechanism and correct intra-abdominal positioning of the bladder neck and proximal urethra. Stress incontinence may also occur secondary to detrusor instability. Patients with stress incontinence that is clinically demonstrable on coughing and do not complain of urinary frequency, urgency, or urge incontinence, do not routinely require urodynamic evaluation prior to surgery. However, VCMG is particularly important in the assessment of cases of stress incontinence with symptoms suggestive of detrusor instability or a history of failed surgical correction.

### History and examination

Important factors in the history are the factors that induce stress incontinence and an assessment of the amount leaked. Associated frequency, urgency and urge incontinence suggest the possibility of stress incontinence due to detrusor instability. Examination may reveal anterior or posterior vaginal wall prolapse, introital atrophy, or urethral mucosal prolapse. These findings may be of significance in the aetiology of stress incontinence. The patient should be asked to cough and perform a Valsava manoeuvre in both the standing and lying positions. The degree of prolapse of the vaginal walls and

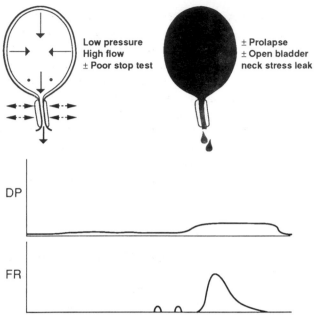

**Fig. 5.2** Genuine stress incontinence.

cervix should be examined and the presence and amount of stress incontinence observed. It is preferable to perform the examination when the patient has a full bladder.

**Urodynamics** (Fig. 5.2)

Patients with stress incontinence usually have a high flow rate (30–60 ml/s), short voiding time and do not leave a postmicturition residual. Cystometry is not necessary in all cases of clinically demonstrable stress incontinence. Indications for urodynamic evaluation are the possibility of associated detrusor instability and a prior history of failed surgery. With VCMG fluoroscopy during filling may reveal opening of the bladder neck and/or descent of the bladder base in the supine or standing positions. In GSI the pressure should not rise above 15 cm $H_2O$ during filling. Cough leak is almost always demonstrable and is often associated with bladder base descent. Voiding is usually rapid and complete with a high flow rate (40−60 ml/s) and low voiding pressure due to reduced outflow resistance. Many of the patients are unable to interrupt micturition due to weakness of the urethral sphincter mechanism.

The amount of urinary leakage that the patient experiences in everyday life may be assessed by performing pad-weighing. More specialised tests, such as urethral profilometry, the fluid bridge test and urethral electrical conductance, have been used to investigate GSI. They are not of benefit in diagnosis and should be reserved for research purposes.

### Treatment

The concept behind the treatment of GSI is to increase the outflow resistance. Pelvic floor exercises and electrical stimulation may help some cases. Surgical treatment is more efficacious and aims to reposition the bladder neck, either by suspension as in the Stamey and Pereyra-Raz procedures, or by open elevation and anterolateral repositioning of the vaginal vault in colposuspension. Approximately 30% of cases may develop detrusor instability in the postoperative period, albeit often temporarily, and this is secondary to the increase in outflow resistance.

## PRIMARY DETRUSOR INSTABILITY

The normal bladder is a compliant structure and the detrusor pressure should not rise during filling, unless overfilled to the point where the subject is in discomfort. An abnormal pressure rise during filling, when the subject is making no attempt to void, is defined by the ICS as detrusor instability. When such a pressure rise is associated with known neurological deficit the alternative name of detrusor hyperreflexia should be used. There are two main patterns of detrusor instability—phasic, or systolic, in which the pressure rises are in a wave form, and hypocompliant in which the pressure rise is linearly related to the filled volume. On occasions there may be combined hypocompliance and phasic contractions. Detrusor instability may develop secondary to bladder outflow obstruction and the commonest case is the elderly male with benign prostatic hypertrophy. Other examples are boys with urethral valves, young males with bladder neck dyssynergia and females after surgical treatment of stress incontinence. When not secondary to outflow obstruction, detrusor instability is defined as idiopathic or primary. The aetiology of primary detrusor instability is not fully understood, but it may be triggered in certain individuals by coughing or giggling, leading to incontinence.

## History and examination

Patients with detrusor instability may complain of frequency, urgency and, if severe, also urge incontinence. They may also have stress incontinence secondary to opening of the bladder neck due to increase in the intravesical pressure. Examination is usually unremarkable, although it is important to check that the bladder is not palpable (suggesting outflow obstruction and secondary detrusor instability). Also, neurological examination might reveal a deficit suggesting a diagnosis of detrusor hyperreflexia. It is therefore important to check that there is no impairment of sensation in the sacral dermatomes, muscle wasting, weakness or disturbance of reflexes in the lower limbs, or decreased anal sphincter tone.

## Urodynamics (Fig. 5.3)

In cases of primary detrusor instability, the free flow rate is characteristically high and the time to maximum flow is reduced (often $< 2$ s). On initial catheterisation it is unusual to find any residual urine. During filling, the pressure rises above 15 cm $H_2O$ and at this point the patient usually complains of urgency and/or impending incontinence. The pattern of unstable detrusor

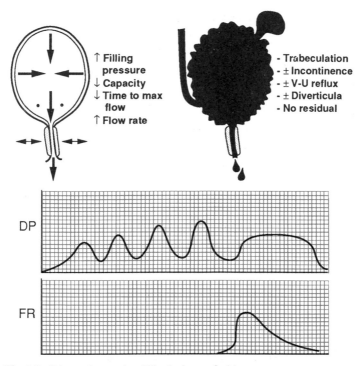

↑ Filling pressure
↓ Capacity
↓ Time to max flow
↑ Flow rate

- Trabeculation
- ± Incontinence
- ± V-U reflux
- ± Diverticula
- No residual

DP

FR

**Fig. 5.3** Primary detrusor instability (or hyperreflexia).

contractions is usually phasic or systolic in appearance (Fig. 5.4) but may on occasions be a linear rise, which is referred to as hypocompliance. Hypocompliance may result from fibrosis of the bladder wall (the so-called plastic bag effect), but also occurs in the neuropathic bladder. Overstretching of the normal bladder to the point where the subject experiences severe pain may induce a hypocompliant pressure rise and this should be avoided. On occasions systolic pressure waves may be superimposed upon a hypocompliant pressure rise. Fluoroscopy of the unstable bladder during filling usually demonstrates trabeculation of the bladder and

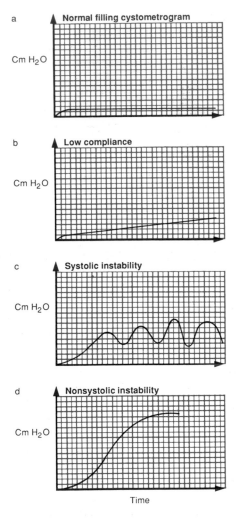

**Fig. 5.4** Patterns of filling detrusor pressure (a) normal subjects and (b) low compliance and detrusor instability.

occasionally diverticula may be seen. Opening of the bladder neck may be seen with pressure rises, particularly in the female, and this may lead to secondary stress incontinence. Vesicoureteric reflux is more common in association with high detrusor pressures and this may be seen on fluoroscopy. Voiding is usually rapid and with a high flow rate and normal voiding pressure. A stop test is not always possible owing to the force of the detrusor contraction, but when successful the $P_{ISO}$ is often high ($> 50$ cm $H_2O$). Patients with primary detrusor instability usually void to completion, but associated diverticula may not empty. Vesicoureteric reflux may occur during voiding, particularly at the time of the stop test when the intravesical pressure is particularly elevated.

## Treatment

It is important for all cases of primary detrusor instability to undergo a cystoscopy to exclude the presence of an irritative lesion such as carcinoma or carcinoma in-situ of the bladder, radiolucent stones, or foreign bodies that might have caused the problem. Appropriate and successful treatment of such conditions should cure detrusor instability. Having excluded an irritative lesion the next therapeutic approach should be bladder training, in which the patient is instructed to make a conscious effort to resist the desire to void and to void only when the bladder feels absolutely full. Such training may be assisted by supplying the patient with 'time and amount' charts since, by careful analysis of their micturition pattern, they may acquire greater insight, thereby helping to resolve the problem. Should bladder training fail to control the symptoms adequately, the next step is to institute drug therapy.

The mechanism of action of the agents used to treat detrusor relies mostly upon their anticholinergic properties, although the modern agents terodiline and oxybutinin also have calcium-channel blocking action. Side effects such as dryness of the mouth and dizziness may be encountered with these drugs due to their anticholinergic properties. The contemporary treatments of choice are terodiline

12.5–25 mg twice daily or oxybutynin 5–10 mg three times a day. Should drug therapy fail to control the symptoms, or cause intolerable side effects, surgical intervention should be considered. There has been a recent vogue for subtrigonal injection of phenol in female patients, but we have now abandoned this due to unacceptable side effects, such as fistula formation, sciatic nerve damage and fibrosis. Subtrigonal phenol injection should be avoided in the male since it often leads to impotence. Our favoured surgical treatment for intractable detrusor instability is the 'clam' enterocystoplasty. Through a suprapubic V incision the bladder is divided in the coronal section down to the trigone, taking care to preserve the ureters. A measured segment of terminal ileum and its mesentery are resected and the bowel opened along its antimesenteric border. The patch of bowel is then sutured to the free edges of the divided bladder. Patients undergoing this operation are warned of the potential necessity for intermittent clean self-catheterisation should the augmented bladder fail to empty satisfactorily.

# 6. Sensory disorders

## INTRODUCTION

Although urodynamic investigations were originally developed to study the 'motor' function of the lower urinary tract, some information can also be acquired on bladder sensation. Indeed, it is now appreciated that the sensory arc of the voiding reflex is important in determining voiding function and may also play a role in the aetiology of detrusor instability. Abnormalities of bladder sensation can be broadly categorised into hypersensitive and hyposensitive disorders.

## Abnormalities

Hypersensitivity of the lower urinary tract may be idiopathic, but is often due to inflammation within the bladder and/or urethra. The commonest cause of hypersensitivity is bacterial cystitis and it is important to ensure that no concurrent infection is present during urodynamics since the test will often exacerbate the condition, may lead to Gram-negative septicaemia and is usually not interpretable due to hypersensitivity.

Other infective processes, such as human papilloma virus infection within the urethra and trigone in females, or urethritis and chronic prostatitis in the male, may also lead to hypersensitivity. Other conditions that lead to inflammation, such as bladder calculus, bladder carcinoma, postradiation cystitis, cyclophosphamide cystitis, chemical cystitis and interstitial cystitis, may also cause hypersensitivity. There is also a rather enigmatic group of patients in whom hypersensitivity exists without evidence of inflammation and these are sometimes referred to as 'urethral syndrome' or 'hypersensitive bladders'. All patients with symptoms suggestive of a hypersensitive disorder should have urine culture, careful cysto-urethroscopy (±biopsy) prior to urodynamic assessment.

Impairment of bladder sensation or 'hyposensitive bladder' is usually due to denervation. The best known cause is spinal cord injury, in which the sensory pathways are interrupted. Pelvic trauma and radical surgery such as Wertheim's hysterectomy and abdominoperineal resection of the rectum may lead to impairment of bladder sensation due to local denervation. There is also a group of predominantly female patients in whom the desire to micturate when the bladder is full is impaired for no apparent reason. These cases void infrequently and have a large capacity bladder without evidence of obstruction or detrusor dysfunction and are sometimes referred to as 'camel bladders'!

Bladder sensation may be assessed using stimulating electrodes introduced per urethram, but such techniques are used for research purposes rather than in routine assessment. Urodynamic tests are not ideal techniques for evaluating sensory disorders, but enable the observer to measure objectively the sensory threshold and to exclude motor disorders.

## HYPERSENSITIVE BLADDER

### Definition

A disorder leading to increase in urinary frequency (±urgency, ±bladder pain), in which cystometry fails to demonstrate a rise in the filling detrusor pressure above 15 cm $H_2O$.

## History and examination

A full history is particularly important in the assessment of hypersensitive disorders of the bladder. Urinary frequency is a prominent symptom and bladder pain, rather than impending incontinence, is the trigger. Urgency may also occur but incontinence is not usually present. Nocturnal frequency is often less than diurnal frequency in hypersensitive bladders. Bladder pain, when present, is usually relieved by voiding. Dysuria may be a symptom and suggests the presence of inflammation in the urethra. Strangury is suggestive of trigonal inflammation. Examination may be unremarkable, but attention should be paid to the urethral meatus, which may be inflamed or show mucosal prolapse. There may also be bladder tenderness both suprapubically and on vaginal examination.

## Urodynamics

Catheterisation may be painful in hypersensitive disorders. The passage of the catheter through the urethra and contact with the bladder mucosa may cause pain of a different nature. In some cases catheterisation may not cause discomfort. The major diagnostic feature of hypersensitivity is a premature first sensation of filling and reduced bladder capacity due to bladder discomfort. The filling pressure and voiding function are usually normal.

## Treatment

All cases of hypersensitive bladder should undergo cystoscopy (± biopsy) and those with normal findings are often improved symptomatically by cystodistension and urethral dilatation. Those cases in whom symptoms persist in spite of this treatment may gain symptomatic relief from intravesical instillation of dimethyl sulphoxide administered at a dose of 20 ml at fortnightly intervals for two months. The treatment of bladder hypersensitivity due to infection or mucosal inflammation is beyond the scope of this book (Fig. 6.1).

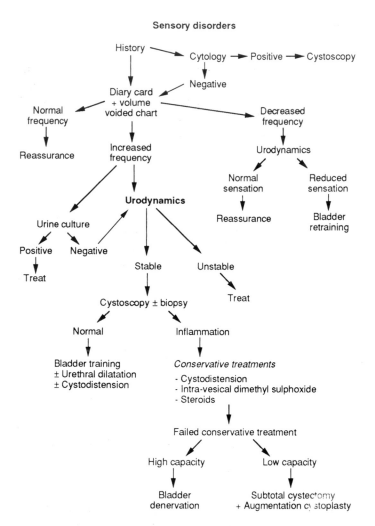

**Fig. 6.1** Flow diagram showing the management of hypersensitive bladder disorder.

# HYPOSENSITIVE BLADDER

## Definition

Impairment of bladder sensation leading to loss, or reduction, of the desire to micturate and hence infrequent micturition and a large bladder capacity. In its early stages this is purely a sensory problem that may lead to detrusor underactivity in the long term due to chronic overdistension of the bladder.

## History and examination

Patients with a hyposensitive bladder may have no complaints apart from loss of the desire to micturate. Infrequent voiding may lead to recurrent urinary tract infection. There may be a previous history of spinal cord/cauda equina injury or pelvic surgery causing bladder denervation. It is unusual for post-traumatic cases to have a selective sensory problem, most being associated with detrusor underactivity. Examination may reveal impairment of sensation in sacral dermatomes.

## Urodynamics

The characteristic urodynamic feature of this condition is an increase in the volume at which the first sensation of filling occurs. In severe cases there may be almost no bladder sensation at all and such cases may have to void without the desire to micturate. In pure hyposensitivity the detrusor function during filling and voiding is normal. Some cases of chronic hyposensitivity who void very infrequently may ultimately develop detrusor muscle failure secondary to chronic over-distension of the bladder.

## Treatment

The treatment of bladder hyposensitivity is bladder training so that the patient is encouraged to void 'by the clock' about six times a day, even though the desire to void may be absent. If such treatment is commenced early in the course of the condition, it should prevent subsequent impairment of detrusor function.

# 7. Bladder contracture

## Definition

A reduction in the functional capacity of the bladder due to fibrotic contracture or carcinoma within the bladder wall. The aetiology of fibrous contracture may be previous irradiation, tuberculosis, chemical cystitis, interstitial cystitis, or schistosomiasis. Fibrotic contracture is preceded by inflammation so that hypersensitivity and contracture may coexist. However, the final stage of the condition may not be accompanied with hypersensitivity.

## History and examination

The patient will usually have a long previous history of the aetiological factors listed above. The predominant complaint is usually urinary frequency by day and night. Urgency and stress incontinence are often present and bladder pain on filling may be a feature if there is concurrent inflammation of the bladder or infiltrating carcinoma. Examination is usually unremarkable, although some suprapubic tenderness may be present.

## Urodynamics

The most striking urodynamic feature of the contracted bladder is the reduction in first sensation volume and bladder capacity. Infiltration of the detrusor muscle by fibrosis may reduce the compliance of the bladder, so that in most cases there is an inappropriate and linear pressure rise during filling. In some cases, fibrosis around the bladder neck prevents closure and hence leads to incontinence during filling after hypocompliant pressure rise, as well as stress incontinence. In a similar way, fibrosis around the ureteric orifices may cause vesicoureteric reflux and in gross cases of bladder contracture the upper tracts act as a reservoir for urine, holding far more than the bladder. In addition to causing hypocompliance during filling, fibrosis of the detrusor muscle layer will also reduce the efficiency of the detrusor during voiding, hence resulting in detrusor underactivity with reduction of the voiding pressure and sometimes compensatory voiding straining. Cases of bladder contracture are best assessed by VCMG. On fluoroscopy, the bladder is generally noted to be unusually spherical and thick-walled. Incontinence and/or vesicoureteric reflux may be noted during filling. Since the contracted bladder is thick-walled, and the efficiency of the detrusor may be compromised, emptying may be incomplete (Fig. 7.1).

## Treatment

Bladder contracture results from a number of different aetiologies which include bladder carcinoma and the sequelae of its treatment by radiotherapy and chronic inflammatory disorders of the bladder. In most cases, treatment will have already failed to halt disease progression and therefore surgical treatment is indicated. The majority of cases of contracture associated with bladder carcinoma are best treated by cystectomy and urinary diversion or bladder reconstruction. Dimethyl sulphoxide is thought to soften collagen, but intravesical instillation of this agent in cases of bladder contracture due to chronic interstitial cystitis has not been shown to have a lasting beneficial effect. Cystodistension under general anaesthetic does not produce long-term symptomatic relief. Most severe cases of fibrotic bladder contracture ultimately require augmentation cystoplasty. The details of various augmentation techniques is beyond the scope of this book. A number of different

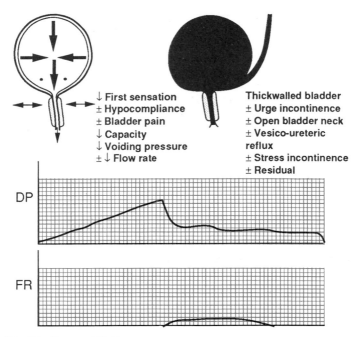

↓ First sensation
± Hypocompliance
± Bladder pain
↓ Capacity
↓ Voiding pressure
± ↓ Flow rate

Thickwalled bladder
± Urge incontinence
± Open bladder neck
± Vesico-ureteric reflux
± Stress incontinence
± Residual

DP

FR

**Fig. 7.1** Contracted bladder.

techniques are now available for bladder augmentation and its orthotopic replacement. Attention has been directed to the prevention of reflux into the uper tracts; by the use of split nipple reimplantation, submucosal tunnelling and the construction of flap valves using intestine as appropriate.

## FURTHER READING

Abrams P H, Feneley R C L, Torrens M J 1983 Urodynamics. Springer, Berlin, Heidelberg, New York

Gosling J A, Dixon J S, Humpherson J R 1983 Functional anatomy of the urinary tract. Churchill Livingstone, London

Mundy A R, Stephenson T P, Wein A J (eds) 1984 Urodynamics— principles, practice and application. Churchill Livingstone, Edinburgh

Turner-Warwick R T, Whiteside C G (eds) 1979 Clinical urodynamics. In: The Urological Clinics of North America, vol 6(1). W B Saunders, Philadelphia

## LIST OF ABBREVIATIONS

| | |
|---|---|
| NANC | non-adrenergic non-cholinergic |
| DSD | detrusor/sphincter dyssynergia |
| ICS | International Continence Society |
| IVUD | intravenous urodynamogram |
| CMG | cystometrogram |
| VCMG | videocystometrogram |
| USCD | ultrasound cystodynamogram |
| UPP | urethral pressure profile |
| VUPP | voiding urethral pressure profile |
| EMG | electromyography |
| GSI | genuine stress incontinence |
| TURP | transurethral prostatectomy |

# Index